The RAT

V. Adam. Del.   Beaupré Sc

Le Mulot, le Rat, la Souris.

The RAT

A PERVERSE MISCELLANY

COLLECTED by BARBARA HODGSON

Ten Speed Press

Berkeley, California

A Kirsty Melville Book

Ten Speed Press
Post Office Box 7123
Berkeley, California 94707

Design by Barbara Hodgson / Byzantium Books

LIBRARY OF CONGRESS CATALOGING-IN-PUBLICATION DATA

The rat : a perverse miscellany / collected by Barbara Hodgson.
    p. cm.
"A Kirsty Melville book"——T.p. verso.
Includes bibliographical references and index.
ISBN 0-89815-926-1
1. Rats—Anecdotes. 2. Rats in literature.   3. Rats—Folklore
I. Hodgson, Barbara, 1955—
QL737.R666R375   1997
599.35'2——DC21   97-6940
                                 CIP

Originally published by Greystone Books, Douglas & McIntyre
First Ten Speed Press printing, 1997
Printed in Hong Kong

ABOVE: *Gustave Doré illustration of the Jean de la Fontaine fable "The City Rat and the Country Rat," 1867.*

RIGHT: *Nineteenth-century English engraving of black water rats.*

FACING PAGE: *Gustave Doré illustration of the Jean de la Fontaine fable "Council of the Rats," 1867.*

FRONTISPIECE: *Nineteenth-century colour engravings of rats and mice. From left to right: le rat perchal, le champagnol, le rat d'eau, le mulot, le rat, la souris.*

CONTENTS

PREFACE

I had never seen a live rat at such close quarters before. Yet there it was, in the obscurity of the night—a seemingly huge brown rat, barely twenty feet away, gnawing on my soap. It must have been the scuffling of its paws along the window sill that woke me up, and it was certainly the long shadows cast by the streetlights outside and the delicate nibbling noises that kept me up. What do you do when confined with a rat in a tiny hotel room? I'll tell you what I did—I flicked on the light, crawled into the farthest corner and proceeded to stare fiercely at the animal. My intense gaze had little or no effect on the affronted rat, but the light did, and it finally went away. This encounter took place on the Greek island of Kos. Greece doesn't have rats, I thought to myself. Greece is a paradise. Greece has colourful fish and friendly cats, but surely not anything as horrible as a rat, and surely not in my pretty little hotel room just steps from the picturesque harbour!

I had never met a live rat until then, though I had seen a number of dead ones in Aleppo, lying about in the alleyways of the old bazaar. They weren't dead from visible causes, such as being run over by a bicycle or a car; they were dead from unknown causes, plumply, unnervingly dead. A plump dead rat is Camus territory, and Camus wrote about the plague. A dead rat is not a pleasant sight.

Later on, I saw rats playing along the banks of the Nile in Cairo. They seemed cute there, although not everyone thought so. Overheard were two English voices exclaiming, "Look how charming, what are they?" and then the cries of disgust when a passer-by identified them as rats.

These are my memories of rats. I am a traveller who long associated rats with exotic lands, the pestilential past and gothic tales such as Edgar Allan Poe's "The Pit and the Pendulum"—the stuff of novels and fertile imaginations out of control. Until recently, that is, after stepping out of my house in a placid

A noble rendering of a rat. Engraving from a drawing by Buffon (Georges-Louis Leclerc, comte de Buffon).

This illustration by Gustave Doré from Histoire pittoresque, dramatique et caricaturale de la sainte Russie, *1854, exemplifies the horror often associated with rats.*

Vancouver suburb and facing a rat gone berserk. The animal was occupied with chasing its own tail and kept this up for at least twenty minutes. I left before it stopped, carrying away with me the realization that rats don't just live in foreign lands of shadow and mystery; they live with us and have done so for a long time.

After my rather uneasy encounters with the rat world, I began to notice that a number of writers, especially travel writers, went out of their way to work rats into their stories. In an account of a trip through West Africa in the 1930s, Graham Greene writes: "That night the rats came leaping into my room like large cats." In Barbara Greene's account of that same trip, she reports: "One of the nuns at Bolahun had most vividly described to us how she had woken up one night to find a rat on her face. A singularly unpleasant experience."

Novelists have frequently been seduced by images of rats, for nothing conjures up a sense of urban horror better. Ian Fleming knew that when he placed James Bond in the sewers of Istanbul in his novel *From Russia with Love*: "Twenty yards away on either side, a thousand rats were looking at Bond. They were sniffing at his scent. Bond imagined the whiskers lifting slightly from their teeth. He had a quick moment of wondering what action they would take if his torch went out." Poe, in "The Pit and the Pendulum," shunned the cityscape and created a world of horror in an Inquisition dungeon and then packed it full of rats: "They swarmed upon me in ever accumulating heaps. They writhed upon my throat; their cold lips sought my own."

Descriptions of rats demand superlatives: they survive falls from the most unbelievable heights, they produce an incredible number of offspring in a year, they eat massive amounts of anything. The rat is not, like the dog, congratulated for its loyalty, or, like the cat, for its intelligence. The words associated with rats fall into the category of the seven deadly sins: they are cunning, voracious, lascivious, evil. The following pages are devoted to rats and their habits and accomplishments, but most of all to centuries of literary and pictorial evocations that show just how deep our fascination for this repellent rodent is.

ACKNOWLEDGEMENTS

I would like to thank everyone who helped me with the research, especially the following people: Barbara Smith, for braving phone calls in foreign languages, for her hours of invaluable research and enthusiasm for the movies and ephemera, and for the interviews with the Toronto and Washington, D.C., rat control departments; Karen Elizabeth Gordon, for more rats than one could ever count; Françoise Giovannangeli, for the precious interviews with the Section and the Service de lutte contre les rongeurs in Paris and for cutting through the red tape at the Bibliothèque Nationale; Janine Giovannangeli, for the tip on Michel Dansel's book and for introducing me to Françoise; Isabelle Swiderski, for hours in the library and help with the French slang; Saeko Usukawa, always on the lookout; Lurdes Silva, for her help with the Portuguese; Sal Nensi, for his help with the Bengali; Doris Shadbolt, for generously allowing me to reprint her observations of the Deshnoke temple in India and for her other rat recollections; Don Stewart of MacLeod's Books in Vancouver, for the Thymo-Cresol ad from the Montreal City Directory and for Dr Chase; Nancy Flight, for her suggestions and her faith in the project; Alex Hass, for the Ben Okri reference; Michael Ondaatje, for suggesting Edwin Arlington Robinson; Brendan Moss, for the loan of Billy; John Atkin, for the loan of the rat letter; Nick Bantock, for the *Century* and *Player* rats; and finally, David, for stoically withstanding all the rat talk.

ABOVE: *This illustration, signed W. Dickes, was part of a series of tea package inserts. It shows the brown, long-tailed and black rat. The back of the card carries informative and amusing descriptions of the animals.*

LEFT: *Gustave Doré illustration of the la Fontaine fable "Un animal dans la lune" ("An animal in the moon").*

ix

French newspaper illustration by L. Tazzini from 1879 depicts sailors as they meet their end and encounter the rats deserting the sinking ship. The caption reads: "Les Rats de Norwège—Il y avait plus de mille rats" ("The Rats of Norway—There were more than a thousand").

THE BROWN RAT.

1. RAT TALK

Few people, rat fanciers excepted, would describe rats as endearing, cute or lovable. Some writers like Martin Hart favour a more magnanimous attitude towards rats, but it is difficult, especially when looking back at the long written record, not to share the revulsion of writers through the ages.

According to the *Barnhart Dictionary of Etymology*, the word *rat* first appeared in Ælfric's vocabulary, in about A.D. 1000. It was used as a place name in 1185. The first time the word *rat* occurs in English literature is in the poem *Piers the Plowman*, written by Chaucer's contemporary William Langland in 1378. The source is the Indo-European word *rəd*, related to the word *red/rod*, "to gnaw" (e.g., the Latin *rodere*, "to gnaw").

The word *rat* has come to be associated with an infinite number of slang phrases and puns. Speakers of many languages have creatively capitalized on the rat's characteristics: long and hairless tail, constant gnawing, voracious appetite, profuse and rapid breeding, and the inevitable association with dirt, disease and vermin. Hence, for English speakers, the vividness of a phrase such as "I smell a rat": that is, to sense something unpleasant while not being able to see it.

The saying that I've encountered most often is the inevitable favourite of impressionists: "I'll get you, you dirty rat," commonly attributed to James Cagney in the film *Angels with Dirty Faces*. In his autobiography, *Cagney on Cagney*, he took great exception to this attribution and categorically denied ever having said it. Which leaves us somewhat at a loss to explain just where it came from. Missing source or not, however, the meaning is clear and the association with gangsters is immediate.

No-one can rest, with rats out at night.
—William Langland, *Piers the Plowman*, 71

"Bogies is rats, and rats is bogies!"
—Bram Stoker, "The Judge's House," *Dracula's Guest and Other Weird Stories*, 25

J.J. Grandville illustration of the la Fontaine fable "Conseil tenu par les rats" ("Council held by the rats").

FACING PAGE: *Nineteenth-century English coloured engraving of brown rats.*

1

Avoir les rats noirs: To be depressed.

Cellar rat: A device from France that has passed into obscurity. Victor Hugo described it best:
Gavroche had just managed to ignite one of those bits of cord dipped in resin which are called *cellar rats*. The *cellar rat,* which emitted more smoke than light, rendered the interior . . . confusedly visible.
—Victor Hugo, *Les Misérables,* 130

Pauvre comme un rat d'église: Poor as a church mouse.

Rat: A pad used to puff out hair: "Next morning, at breakfast, Sin Saxon was as beautifully ruffled, ratted, and crimped . . . as ever."—Mrs Whitney quoted in the *Century Encyclopedia*

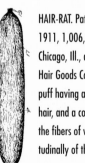

HAIR-RAT. Patent from October 17, 1911, 1,006,022. Charles N. Stephens, Chicago, Ill., assignor to The Sanitary Hair Goods Company. "A rat, roll or puff having a center composed of curly hair, and a covering of crimped wool the fibers of which are disposed longitudinally of the rat."—*The Official Gazette of the U.S. Patent Office,* 1911

A Rat Vocabulary

★ *Irish rats rhymed to death:* A reference to the attempt to get rid of rats by creating and reciting poetical charms. The Irish were fond of using rhymes as charms to banish unwanted visitors.
I was never so berhymed since Pythagoras' time,
that I was an Irish rat, which I can hardly remember.
—William Shakespeare, *As You Like It,* Act III, Scene II

★ *Like a drowned rat:* Soaking wet; looking exceedingly dejected.

★ *Mall rats:* A recent phrase used to describe youths who cluster in shopping malls.

★ *Money rat:* In China,
The rat is associated with money; when you hear a rat scrabbling around for food at night, it is said to be "counting money." *Money-rat* is a disparaging way of referring to a miser.—Wolfram Eberhard, *A Dictionary of Chinese Symbols,* 246–47

★ For more about rats and money, we have only to turn to Freud's notebooks and the case of the Rat Man:
Nov. 29.—When at our first interview I told him my fees he said to himself, "For each *krone* a rat for the children." Now *"Ratten"* ["rats"] really meant to him *"Raten"* ["installments"]. He pronounced the words alike . . . He now pays in rats.—Rat currency.—Freud quoted in Peter Gay, *The Freud Reader,* 332

★ *Nestectomy:* The archaeological dissection of a rat's nest.—from Stephen Kreider Yoder, "Rats' nests yield store of tiny domestic treasures," *Wall Street Journal,* March 25, 1995

★ *Rat:* A bread thief in the metaphorical slang of Victor Hugo's criminal world.
—from Victor Hugo, *Les Misérables,* 158

★ *Rat* (as explained by Balzac):
A perversity now forgotten, but common enough in the early years of the century, was the luxury known as a rat. The word, already outmoded, was applied to a child of ten or eleven, a supernumerary at some theatre, generally the Opera, formed by some rake for infamy and vice. A rat was a kind of infernal page, a female urchin to whom everything was forgiven.

A rat could take whatever it pleased; it was best distrusted as a dangerous animal, it introduced an element of gaiety into life . . . A rat was a costly indulgence: it brought neither honour, nor profit, nor pleasure; the fashion for rats faded so completely that few people today knew this intimate detail of the life of elegance before the Restoration.—Honoré de Balzac, *A Harlot High and Low*, 27

★ *Rat or rat-fink:* An informer, a despicable person, or general low-life.
"You pasty-faced, skunk-gutted, ricket-ridden little rats!"
—Carson McCullers, *The Heart Is a Lonely Hunter*, 216

★ *Rat hole:* A squalid dive.
The Hôtel X was a vast, grandiose place with a classical façade, and at one side a little, dark doorway like a rat-hole which was the service entrance.—George Orwell, *Down and Out in Paris and London*, 49

★ *Rat race:* Once a term meaning "a dance of a low-grade nature," it now means the endless treadmill of trying to get ahead:
How long is a rat race? A moderate distance would be 1.6 kilometres a night, according to Carl Cotman of the University of California, who works with the animals. Athletic rats will cover about eight kilometres a night—and their brains have higher levels of neurotrophins, which retard brain-cell aging. "Get out there and do something," urges the director of the Institute for Brain, Aging and Dementia.—Michael Kesterton, "The patter of little feet," *Globe and Mail*, July 17, 1995

★ *Rats desert a sinking ship:* One of the more common characteristics of rats. The second their shelter becomes insecure, they leave. Another version of this phrase appears in a Victorian dictionary:
Rats and mice have generally been considered sacred animals. Among the Scandinavian and Teutonic peoples they were regarded as the souls of the dead . . . It is not unlikely that the saying "Rats desert a falling house," applied originally to the crumbling ruin of the body from which the soul fled.—Bishop Hatto quoted in Robert Gordon Latham, *A Dictionary of the English Language*, 705

Raternity: From the French *raternité*, coined by Michel Dansel to describe the close association between rats that allows them to communicate survival details such as the appearance of a new poison.—from Michel Dansel, *Nos Frères les Rats*

Rat pack: Used to describe a rebellious or noncomformist group. One example includes the Hollywood Rat Pack consisting of Frank Sinatra, Sammy Davis Jr, Peter Lawford and Dean Martin.

Rats of Montsouris: A term that refers to a fictional gang of burglars in the 14th arrondisement of Paris. Nestor Burma, the dynamic chief of the Fiat Lux Detective Agency, has a rendezvous with a tattooed, fellow ex-POW in Montmartre and discovers he's now part of this seedy gang.—from Léo Malet, *The Rats of Montsouris*

The Rats of Rangoon: Name used by Wing Commander Lionel Hudson of the RRAF to describe the POWs in Burmese prison camps in his WWII story *The Rats of Rangoon*.

Rat wrangler: A rat trainer for the movies.—Allison Mayes, *Calgary Herald,* February 6, 1995

To have a rat in the garret: An archaic phrase indicating that someone has a screw loose; that is, behaves erratically. —from the *Century Encyclopedia*

To take a rat by the tail: An antiquated French colloquialism from the time of Louis XVII, *prendre un rat par la queue,* meaning to cut the string of a purse while stealing it to avoid spilling the contents.—*Brewer's Dictionary of Phrase & Fable,* 1040

Other rats, real and otherwise:
Alexandria rat: native to Alexandria
Bamboo rat: native to India
Bandicoot rat: native to India
Hare-tailed rat
Hedgehog rat
Maori rat: black rat naturalized to New Zealand
Mountain rat: lives in the Rocky Mountains and is aka the *Pack rat*
Muskrat
Pharaonic rat: ichneumon
Pouched rat
Water rat

★ *Rats!:* An exclamation of dismay or disappointment.

★ *Rat's tail:*

> Jan 3.— . . . After I had told him that a rat was a penis, *via* worm (at which point he at once interpolated "a little penis")—rat's tail.—Freud quoted in Peter Gay, *The Freud Reader,* 346

★ *Rattrap:* Usually refers to a structure that is unsafe, ready to be condemned. Noël Coward, however, had another definition in one of his plays, where he describes the state of an unhappy relationship:

> We should never have married, however much in love we thought we were; I realize it now . . . we're like two rats in a trap, fighting, fighting, fighting.—Noël Coward, *The Rat Trap,* 50

★ *Roi de rats:* King of Rats, originally used in France to describe someone who lived off the avails of others. *King Rat,* the head of the pack (human or rat), is the title of the James Clavell novel about such a character.

★ *Slope rats:* A recent term used to describe snowboarders.

★ *Tête de rat:* Used by Georges Simenon in one of his novels to describe a thin, anxious-looking man waiting to see Inspector Maigret at his office at the Quai des Orfèvres:

> There was only one man, that morning, in the [room they called] Purgatory, and Maigret noted that he appeared to be the kind of man one usually called "rat head." He was rather thin. His receding forehead was crowned by a foamy mass of red hair. He must have had blue or violet eyes and his nose seemed to jut out as much as his chin receded.—Georges Simenon, *Maigret à l'école,* 8–9

★ *To rat:* Comes from the rats' habit of jumping ship if the going got rough. Strikebreakers are often referred to as rats.

★ *To rat on:* To inform on someone. A "stoolie" or "stool-pigeon" is also a rat.

★ *To smell a rat:* To sense something concealed which is mischievous or harmful. The allusion is to a cat *smelling* a rat, while unable to *see* it.

Nineteenth-century coloured engraving from France.

Comparisons

If now I think—at this most far away moment of a breakdown, a physical and moral disgust—of the pink tail of a rat in the snow, it seems to share *in the intimacy* of "that which is"; a slight uneasiness clutches my heart. And certainly I know that the intimacy of M., who is dead, was like the tail of a rat, *lovely as the tail of a rat!* I knew already that the intimacy of things is death.—Georges Bataille, *The Impossible: A Story of Rats*, 54

Endearments

F. O. Matthiessien, who was a cultural historian, nicknamed the Devil, had a long correspondence with his friend Russell Cheney, the Rat. Matthiessen sent this letter to Cheney on November 4, 1924:

Dearest Rat,

While we are on the subject of names you don't know how long it took me to get used to that one. If there is anything on earth that makes my blood cold, it is a rat. Ugh! How I loathe them! But as a name, I knew you liked it. It was short and convenient, and pleasant sounding when I could forget its meaning. So I gradually got used to it; and then came the sketch of the San Marco canvas with a Rat bent in all humility before it. That was slick, and since then I've forgotten my first prejudice. You damn black Rat—how I love you.—F.O. Matthiessen and Russell Cheney, *Rat & The Devil*, 45

The bailiff of the Palace was a kind of amphibious magistrate, a sort of bat of the judicial order, a mixture of rat and bird, judge and soldier.—Victor Hugo, *The Hunchback of Notre Dame*, 44

You are consorting with the scum of the earth, and you *know what you are doing*. To save your own skin you accept help from an inhuman beast in the form of a man. He is so filthy a creature that we cannot be in the same room with him without being polluted. You cannot fail to see all that, as I say. You are a rat—yes, a far worse rat because you are an *intelligent* rat!

—Wyndham Lewis, *Monstre Gai*, 185

Gustave was the Bear. His sister Caroline was the Rat—"your dear rat," "your faithful rat" she signs herself; "little rat," "Ah, rat, good rat, old rat," "old rat, naughty old rat, good rat, poor old rat" he addresses her—but Gustave was the Bear.—Julian Barnes, *Flaubert's Parrot*, 49

He gave us also the example of the philosopher, who, when he thought most seriously to have withdrawn himself unto a solitary privacy . . . was notwithstanding his uttermost endeavours to free himself from all untoward noises, surrounded and environed about so with the barking of curs, bawling of mastiffs, bleating of sheep, prating of parrots, tattling of jackdaws, grunting of swine, girning of boars, . . . rantling of rats.—François Rabelais, *Gargantua and Pantagruel*, 152

Gustave Doré illustration from Gargantua and Pantagruel. *François Rabelais (1495–1553), a French writer and anatomist, published* Gargantua *in 1532 and* Pantagruel *in 1533.*

Rat Names

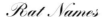

"In fact," the tall boy continued, "just sit comfy there and I'll do it right here with my fingernail file. You won't even need to use your Blue Cross. What'd'ya think of that plan, Ratso?"

"The name is Rizzo."

"That's what I said, Ratso."—James Leo Herlihy, *Midnight Cowboy*, 94

What's in a name? That name's whole history. I am not Rat Man, by preference, for nothing. *L'homme des rats*. The man of the rats. *L'homme aux rats*. The man with rats. *L'homme rat*. The man rat.—Paul West, *Rat Man of Paris*, 69

Miscellaneous

Having talked of Grainger's "Sugar-Cane," I mentioned to him Mr. Langton's having told me, that this poem, when read in manuscript at Sir Joshua Reynolds' had made all the assembled wits burst into a laugh, when, after much blank verse pomp, the poet began a new paragraph thus:

"Now, Muse, let's sing of *rats*."

And what increased the ridicule was, that one of the company, who slyly overlooked the reader, perceived that the word had been originally *mice*, and had been altered to *rats*, as more dignified.—James Boswell, *The Life of Samuel Johnson*, 621

Wordplay

"To star rats is simply to star rats," Lozano says. "As a phrase, it has no strength because it doesn't teach you anything new and because no one can really 'star' rats. You are left the way you started, which is the problem with palindromes."

"Right," says Pardo Illa.

"But if you say it in the singular, everything changes. To star *a* rat isn't the same as to star rats."

"It doesn't seem very different."

"Because it's no longer valid as a palindrome," Lozano says. "Put it in the singular and everything changes, something new is born, it's no longer a mirror, or it's a different mirror, showing you something you don't know."

"What's new about it?"

"Well, to star a rat gives you Tara Rats."

"Tara?"

"It's a name, but all names isolate and define. Now you know there's a rat called Tara, a leader among rats. They all must have names, that's for sure, but now there's one called Tara."

"And what have you gained with that?"

"I don't know, but let me carry on. Last night I realized that by changing just one letter in *rats* you have all the letters that make up *salt*. New things, you see: rats, salt."

"Not so new," Yarará says, listening from a distance. "They've always been there, the rats, the salt."

"All right," Lozano says, "but it points to a way, maybe to the only way of getting rid of them."—Julio Cortázar, "Tara," *Unreasonable Hours*, 32–33

James had been surprised to find that the Dump had its own TV, but it turned out to be rat TV, which was worse than nothing. He couldn't understand the squeaky rat language, of course."
—Peter Dickinson, *A Box of Nothing*, 30

Anything like the sound of a rat
Makes my heart go pit-a-pat!
—Robert Browning, "The Pied Piper of Hamelin"

A nineteenth-century engraving of two rats.

2. AROUND THE WORLD

Travel is an activity shared by many animals, but none more than rats and humans. One of the many benefits that humans have bestowed upon the rat is new and faster methods of transportation. No more anxious moments following Mongol hordes, gone the uncertainties of cadging lifts on the backs of elephants traversing the Indian subcontinent, finished are the days of sea-sickness and never-changing horizons in the holds of merchant ships—no, now there are jet planes and trains, not to mention sleeker, faster ships to whisk entire populations to new and fertile ground. Rats, like people, haven't always been global citizens. There is much controversy, but many agree that the plague-carrying black rat probably arrived in Europe around the time of the Crusades. And when it did arrive, it was with man's help. The spread of the black rat and the subsequent appearance of plague throughout the Middle East and Europe isn't much chronicled—it took a while to put two and two together—but once the rat and, especially, its prodigious population expansion were noticed, imaginations caught on fire and the rat began to appear in many historians' accounts and travellers' tales.

Like humans, rats appear almost everywhere: from Alaska to Liberia, from Seattle to New Guinea, showing pretty much the same taste for moderate climate, reliable shelter and plentiful sustenance. Along with their ubiquitous presence, rats have a keen sense of survival and a tourist's sensibilities.

Thence we turned and coasted up the Adriatic, its shores swimming in an atmosphere of amber, rose, and aquamarine; we lay in wide land-locked harbours, we roamed through ancient and noble cities, until at last one morning, as the sun rose royally behind us, we rode into Venice down a path of gold. O, Venice is a fine city, wherein a rat can wander at his ease and take his pleasure!—Kenneth Grahame, *The Wind in the Willows*, 213

FACING PAGE: *Photograph by Stephen Dalton/ NHPA.*
ABOVE: *Illustration by Ernest Shepard from* The Wind in the Willows *by Kenneth Grahame, 1908.*
LEFT: *J. J. Grandville's illustration of the la Fontaine tale "Le rat et l'huitre" ("The Rat and the Oyster") shows the rat ready to embark on his travels.*

By [1284] the rat had penetrated into England. It had reached Ireland some time before this, where it was the "foreign" or "French" mouse, "ean francach." Our authorities tell us that in Ireland, even until very recent times, everything foreign was called "francach," or French.—

Hans Zinsser, *Rats, Lice and History*, 198–99

DANISH/NORWEGIAN: rotte

SWEDISH: råtta

FINNISH: rotta

ESTONIAN: rott

LATVIAN: zurka

GAELIC: radan

ICELANDIC: rotta

CORNISH: logosen rräs

IRISH: francach

GERMAN: Ratte

POLISH: szczur

CZECH: krysa

WELSH: llygoden fawr

DUTCH: rat

HUNGARIAN: patkány

SLOVENE: podgana

RUMANIAN: sobolan

SERBO-CROAT: paçov

FRENCH: rat, rate

LATIN: mus

BOSNIAN: paçov

ESPERANTO: rato

BASQUE: arratoi

ITALIAN: ratto, topo

TURKISH: sıçan

AZERBA... siçovul

PORTUGUESE: rato

SPANISH: rata

ALBANIAN: mi i math

KURDISH: bele...

GREEK: aroure'os

HEBREW: achbrosch

PER... mo...

ARABIC: al-far

ARABIC: al-far

HAUSA: bera

SOMALI: jiir

SWAHILI: panya

KIKUYU: mbĩa ndembei

AFRIKAANS: rot

SESOTHO: tweba

ZULU: impuku

RATS AROUND THE WORLD

From The P&O Pocket Book of 1908. *The shipping lines (marked in red) represent convenient travel routes for both humans and rats.*

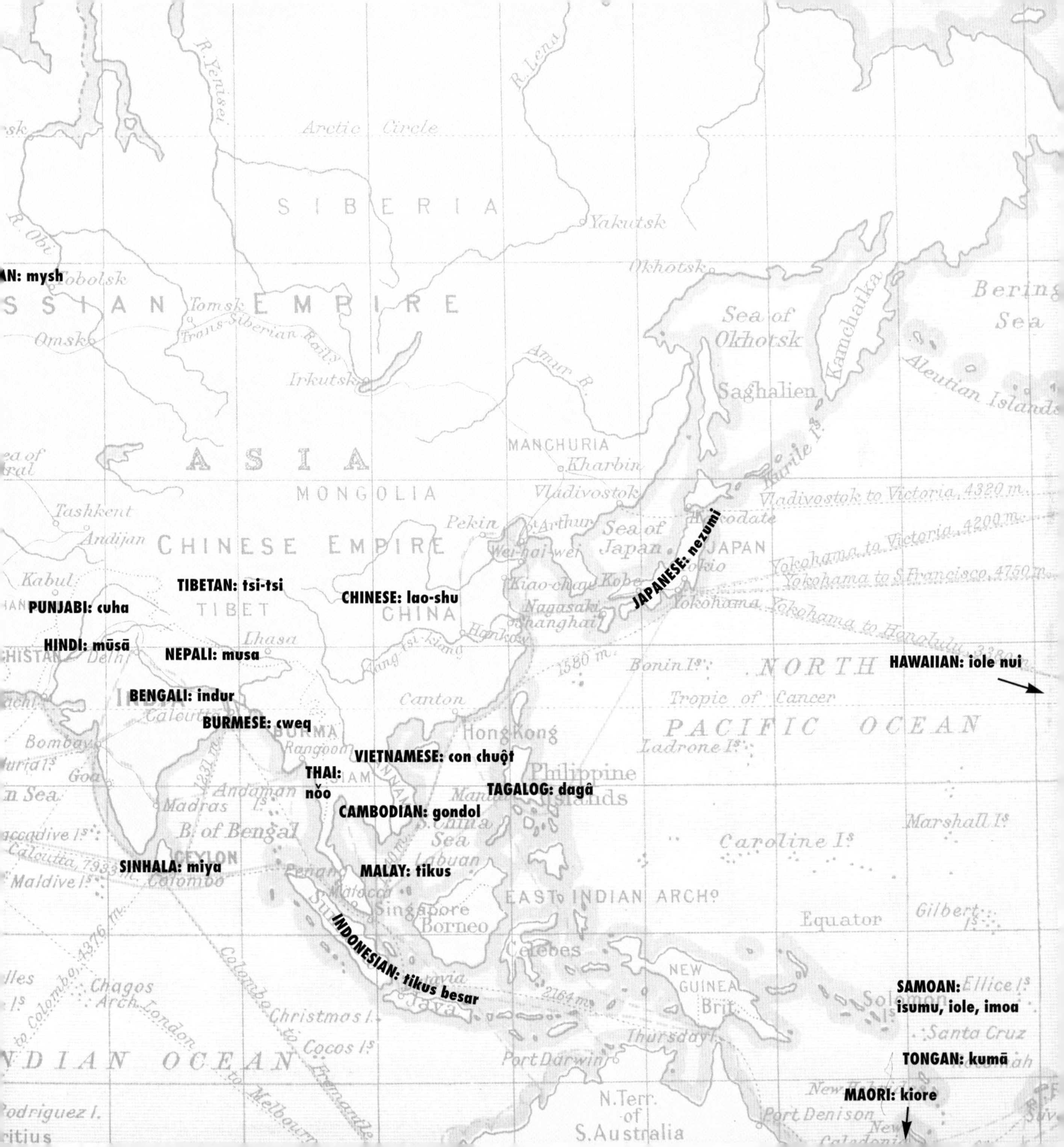

AN: mysh
TIBETAN: tsi-tsi
PUNJABI: cuha
CHINESE: lao-shu
JAPANESE: nezumi
HINDI: mūsā
NEPALI: musa
HAWAIIAN: iole nui
BENGALI: indur
BURMESE: cweq
VIETNAMESE: con chuột
THAI:
nǒo
TAGALOG: dagâ
CAMBODIAN: gondol
SINHALA: miya
MALAY: tikus
INDONESIAN: tikus besar
SAMOAN:
isumu, iole, imoa
TONGAN: kumā
MAORI: kiore
SIBERIA
SSIAN EMPIRE
ASIA
MONGOLIA
MANCHURIA
CHINESE EMPIRE
TIBET
CHINA
INDIA
BURMA
JAPAN
NORTH
PACIFIC OCEAN
NDIAN OCEAN
EAST INDIAN ARCH^o
Arctic Circle
Tropic of Cancer
Equator
Sea of Okhotsk
Bering Sea
Sea of Japan
Philippine Islands
Borneo
Celebes
NEW GUINEA
Java
Ceylon
B. of Bengal
Hong Kong
Canton
Pekin
Yakutsk
Okhotsk
Kamchatka
Saghalien
Aleutian Islands
Kurile I^s.
Kharbin
Vladivostok
Irkutsk
Tomsk
Omsk
Tobolsk
Tashkent
Andijan
Kabul
Delhi
Lhasa
Calcutta
Bombay
Goa
Madras
Colombo
Rangoon
Singapore
Malacca
Penang
Labuan
Manila
Shanghai
Nagasaki
Kobe
Tokio
Yokohama
Hakodate
Bonin I^s.
Ladrone I^s.
Caroline I^s.
Marshall I^s.
Gilbert I^s.
Ellice I^s.
Santa Cruz
Solomon
Thursday I.
Port Darwin
N.Terr. of S.Australia
Port Denison
New Caledonia
Chagos Arch.
Christmas I.
Cocos I^s.
Rodriguez I.
Maldive I^s.
Laccadive I^s.
Andaman I^s.
Trans-Siberian Railway
Amur R.
R. Yenisei
R. Lena
R. Obi
Yang-tsi-kiang
Vladivostok to Victoria, 4320 m.
Yokohama to Victoria, 4200 m.
Yokohama to S.Francisco, 4750 m.
Yokohama to Honolulu, 3380 m.
Calcutta, 7933 m.
Colombo to Fremantle
Colombo, 4376 m.
2164 m.
1580 m.
1231 m.

Newspaper clipping showing an invasion of rats in Australia, 1879.

CANADA

"It's funny. People who phone to complain say they have seen rats, but they are never coming from their yards. They are coming from their neighbors. It's always the neighbors' problem."
—Angelo Kouris, senior environmental health officer for the city of Vancouver, quoted in the Vancouver *Province*, November 8, 1995

BUDGET CUTTING LETS RATS RUN FREE

According to newspaper reporter John Barber, Toronto's public health department received more than 1,200 rat complaints in 1994, but due to budget cuts they will be unable to respond to the complaints.—from John Barber, *Globe and Mail*, March 16, 1995

Arabia

The jerboa*, or spring rat, is a small aery creature in the wide waterless deserts, of a pitiful beauty.—C.M. Doughty, *Passages from Arabia Deserta*, 100

Borneo

A typical case of good intentions gone awry occurred in Sarawak . . . Here the spraying of homes with DDT not only killed mosquitoes but cockroaches. Cats returned to the sprayed homes, ate the poisoned cockroaches and died. Free of predators, the Malaysian field rat, a carrier of plague and typhus, overran the mosquito-free villages. Fearing an outbreak of plague, the WHO eventually asked the Royal Air Force to drop cats by parachutes over the isolated villages.—Andrew Nikiforuk, *The Fourth Horseman*, 24

Canada.

Alberta

One of the pleasures of growing up in Alberta came from the assurance that the province was "rat-free." Indeed, Alberta's status as a rat-free province is so striking that it has been the subject of many newspaper and magazine articles. One such article described the intolerance of health officials towards the rats that crossed the border into Alberta in 1950. They created a no-rats land "25 km long and 500 km wide, from Cold Lake in the north to the U.S. border in the south." As Michael Dolinski, head of Alberta Agriculture's rat control program put it, "every rat that ends up in the province, ends up dead."—from Mary Nemeth, *Maclean's*, August 8, 1994

China

An old Chinese proverb, "One rat surpasses three chickens," has found new meaning in China. Several newspaper reporters licked their chops over the

---

* *A silhouette of the jerboa was the symbol for the WWII British Eighth Army, informally known as "the Desert Rats." They operated mainly in the deserts of Egypt and Libya.*

discovery of a new restaurant, the Jia Lu, in Guangzhou (Canton), China. The Jia Lu, which means "super deer" in Chinese, specializes in rat meat. One article titled "Range-fed rats top Guangzhou menu" listed selections on the menu:

Rat with chestnut and duck, lotus seed rat stew, black bean rat, deep-fried lemon rat, rat soup (with potatoes and onions), braised rat with roast pork and garlic, snakes and rat, a pair of rats wrapped in lotus leaves and rat satay with vermicelli.—Peter Goodspeed, *Toronto Star*, October 27, 1992

Unlike the rat, the mouse plays little part in Chinese symbolism, perhaps because it does not do so much harm; perhaps also because both creatures have the same name in Chinese (*shu*). When a distinction must be made, the rat is called "old mouse" (*lao shu*), or "big mouse" (*da shu*).—Wolfram Eberhard, *A Dictionary of Chinese Symbols*, 246–47

Egypt

In Egypt the rat symbolized utter destruction, and also wise judgment, the latter because rats always choose the best bread.—*Brewer's Dictionary of Phrase & Fable*, 754

While we were there [Bir-es-Sidd], a caravan arrives from the opposite direction: the gorge is very narrow; congestion of camels and people; everyone has to dismount and lead his camel by the halter. We go on foot for a time because of the difficulty of the trail: it is strewn with the carcasses of camels; they have their skins, but are completely gutted. This is the work of rats: the hide, dried and stretched by the sun, is intact, but has been gnawed from within until it is no thicker than an onion-skin; it covers the skeleton which itself is scarred with scratches made by rodents' teeth. Innumerable rat-holes in the desert.—Gustave Flaubert, *Flaubert in Egypt: A Sensibility on Tour*, 184

WATCHING POPULAR NEWSROOM SITCOM IS LIKE SWALLOWING PUTRID RATS
—Chinese newspaper headline quoted in *Montreal Gazette*, March 8, 1992

I seen a Chinese one time, related the doughty narrator, that had little pills like putty and he put them in the water and they opened, and every pill was something different. One was a ship, another was a house, another was a flower. Cooks rats in your soup, he appetisingly added, the Chinese does.—James Joyce, *Ulysses*, 549

CAIRO
In present-day Cairo, one Egyptian may say to another: "kubbah"—"a plague on you," and the other may reply: "kubbatyn"—"two plague boils on you!"—Michael W. Dols, *The Black Death in the Middle East*, 120

13

I remembered the first live rat I ever saw. I had returned with my brother from a revue in Paris to a famous hotel on the left bank near the Luxembourg. It was about one o'clock in the morning; my brother went upstairs first; lalloping behind him, like a small rabbit, went a rat. I could hardly believe my eyes as I followed them; it didn't go with the dapper lounge, the rather wealthy international guests. But I wasn't drunk; I could see quite distinctly the rough brown fur on its neck. I suppose one of the million or two rats in Paris was reconnoitering. Its appearance had a premeditated sinister air. One thought of the first Uhlans appearing at the end of a Belgian country road.—Graham Greene, *Journey without Maps*, 157–58

PARIS

Rats (*gaspards* in the sewermen's argot) were both a nuisance and a serious health hazard. One sewerman estimated in 1897 that each sewerman killed two hundred to three hundred rats annually. When cornered, the rats turned vicious. They could jump and inflict nasty wounds on the hands and face.—Donald Reid, *Paris Sewers and Sewermen*, 150

By 1884, there were other places besides the Souris where lesbians used to meet: the Hanneton in the Rue Pigalle and the Rat Mort in the Place Pigalle. It was possible to lunch there, extremely badly, for two francs. "They have to justify the price," wrote Oscar Wilde, who did not repeat the experience.—Philippe Jullian, *Montmartre*, 94

Many people, and especially women, consider rats to be repulsive creatures, which does not, however, prevent them from flaunting the skins of these animals, which in Paris are caught in incredible numbers for this very purpose, in the form of kid gloves.
—Schlegel quoted in Martin Hart, *Rats*, 32

FACING PAGE: *The front and back of a postcard from the Montmartre restaurant Le Rat Mort.* THIS PAGE: *The menu from the same restaurant. All images from Le Rat Mort reproduced with permission of Le Musée de Montmartre, Paris.*

*John Player and Sons of England issued
colour cards on an infinite variety of
subjects. This one featured the black rat.*

FACING PAGE: *Worshippers in the
Jain temple of Deshnoke. James L.
Stanfield/National Geographic. By
permission of* National Geographic.

Germany

The year 1498 . . . was a severe plague year in Germany, and there were
so many rats in Frankfurt that an attendant was stationed for several hours
each day on a bridge in the town and directed to pay a pfennig for every
rat brought in. The attendant cut off the tail of the rat—probably as a
primitive method of accounting—and threw the bodies into the river.
—Hans Zinsser, *Rats, Lice and History*, 192

Great Britain

Rats indeed take some getting used to. There are said to be as many rats
as human beings even in England in the large towns, but the life they lead
is subterranean. Unless one goes down into the sewers, haunts the huge
rubbish dumps which lie past the waste building lots under a thin fume of
smoke, one is unlikely to meet a rat. It needs an effort of imagination in
Piccadilly Circus to realise that for every passing person, there is a rat in
the tunnels underneath.—Graham Greene, *Journey without Maps*, 157

India

Due to its sheer numbers, the rat is a visible part of life in India. Rats are sometimes depicted in statues at the feet of the elephant god Ganesh and rats are
worshipped at the curious Jain temple at Deshnoke in northwestern India about
thirty kilometres from the city of Jodhpur.

November 24 from Bikaner (in Rajasthan)

Then, 18 miles from Bikaner to Karniji (Red) temple at Deshnoke,—small
desert village—typical moment of dusky twilight as night gets ready to
drop down—drum beating steadily as we enter outer court—we notice
chipmunks scuttling across yard and overhead wires—no, my god, rats!
Inside the compound, inner sanctuary, everywhere, thousands of rats. They
flow in continuous stream over piles of grain put out to feed them along
perimeter "arcade." I have bare feet—rats run over them—droppings thick
on ground. Ceremony going on in inner sanctum involves continuous drum

beating, waving of flaming torches, priest smearing vermilion on our foreheads as procession draws us in and down into sanctuary. Jack and I cling to each other as we move forward. Capt Singh (a Jain) has taken off all leather—coat and sandals as well as belt—he bows down to touch floor with his head, participating in the general fervour!! Anomaly—can this be the cultivated sensitive man who has been our wonderful guide for the last couple of days? The saint whose shrine this is, Karni Mata, a miracle worker—when a child brought to her for healing died, she asked that henceforth he be re-born as a rat—so rats do not stray outside the temple and are free of plague when it hits elsewhere. That is the story—have I got it straight?—anyway the rats are sacred here.—Doris Shadbolt, unpublished travel journal, 1974–75

[In India] houses were rat-paradises . . . In the small city of Belgaum one house of three rooms and a verandah sheltered twelve adults, three children, four buffaloes, six bullocks, one goat, one dog, and three fowls. In a three-room grocery shop and house occupied by six Moslems and two ineffectual cats, 197 rats were caught.—Geddes Smith, *Plague on Us*, 321

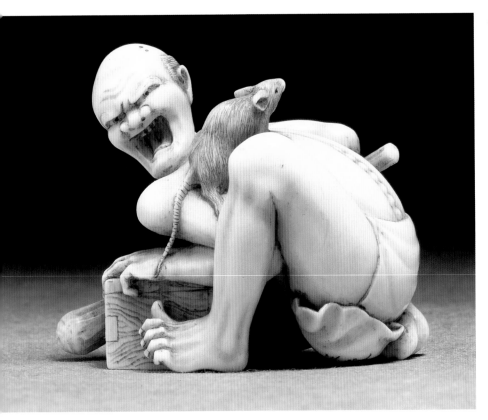

"Thwarted Rat Catcher," a nine-teenth-century netsuke by Masanari. By courtesy of the Board of Trustees of the Victoria & Albert Museum, 529-1904

Japan

In one room of every Japanese house is the domestic altar, kamidana, or sacred shrine, a wooden Shinto temple in miniature, in which, among other things, are kept little tablets bearing the names of the gods, before which the master of the house every day performs his devotions. The space between the boarded and papered ceiling and the roofs of houses is usually inhabited by rats, which at night visit the sleeping-rooms, devour the stearine candles, and otherwise make themselves troublesome.—Philip T. Terry, *Terry's Guide to the Japanese Empire*, i

In an article in the *Globe and Mail*, Miho Yoshikawa describes Tokyo's "hidden problem." Rats abound out of sight thanks to the existence of air spaces in many city buildings used for high-tech wiring and for earthquake resistance. The rats are causing much havoc and are blamed for gnawing through wires and disabling elevators, bank machines and water systems. About 130 pest control companies operate in Tokyo, but health officials wish to preserve the idea that Tokyo is one of the cleanest cities in the world and refuse to provide rat population statistics.—from Miho Yoshikawa, *Globe and Mail*, November 28, 1994

Liberia

I remembered the rats of Monrovia were mentioned. Yes. And, of course, it also said that no steps were taken against plague, that nothing was organised to prevent it spreading and that there was no medical supervision whatsoever of boats touching the Liberian coast. I listened to the rats rushing round my hut, and remembered that plague is carried by rats.

I spent the whole night sitting up in bed frankly terrified. My hands moved round the edge of my bed, continuously tucking in my mosquito-net. I had a fearful idea that if the rats were hungry they might bite through the net, and start nibbling my toes.—Barbara Greene, *Too Late to Turn Back*, 48

Madagascar

Unfortunately we did not have this room to ourselves. Beside the lavatory was a huge hole in the floor, part of the establishment's ingenious plumbing. And through this hole, each night, came a family of the noisiest and most brazen rats I have ever met. When I first heard them I switched on my torch . . . and saw one eating our loaf of breakfast bread and two sitting on their hindlegs by my rucksack, pulling a bar of chocolate out of a side-pocket. When I shone the light on them and shouted threateningly they did not bolt, like properly brought up rats, but squeaked abusively at me and continued to pull. They were incorrigible; we had to learn to live with them.—Dervla Murphy, *Muddling Through in Madagascar*, 246–47

Poland

There's no reason to fear nationalistic overtones. True, we haven't forgotten that the Polish word for rat is *szczur*—we jokingly call one another *szczur*, or, more affectionately *szczurzyca*—but obviously we're not Polish rats. There's no such thing and never was, any more than there are Portuguese or Hungarian rats . . . Still, there's something Polish about us—in this region, undoubtedly. For instance, our taste for dill pickles and caraway seed.—Günter Grass, *The Rat*, 277

JAVA

Attempts have also been made to involve an entire population in the drive to exterminate rats. In Java, for instance, all those applying for a marriage licence were made to supply twenty-five rats' tails. The manufacture of artificial rats' tails (which were almost impossible to distinguish from the genuine article) blossomed into a flourishing industry. The authorities then asked for twenty-five dead rats, whereupon the Javanese began to breed them.—Martin Hart, *Rats*, 143

THE PHILIPPINES

Thomas Y. Canby described a failed effort in the Philippines to sell tinned rat meat. The product was called STAR, RATS backwards. The lack of success, however, didn't prevent others from considering the possibility of putting a rat sausage on the market.—from Thomas Y. Canby, "The Rat: Lapdog of the Devil," *National Geographic*, July 1977, 69

VLADIVOSTOK A NIGHTMARE: CITY OVERRUN BY CROOKS, RATS AND CORRUPTION

Vladivostok, Russia—Strange and frightening things keep happening in this crumbling Pacific coastal city, a grey concrete metropolis where the roads are choked with secondhand Japanese cars, the sidewalks are strewn with dead rats, the harbors are filled with rusting ships—and the politics are as dirty as the water.—Howard Witt, *Winnipeg Free Press*, November 22, 1994

SPAIN

DEAD RATS AMONG DEBRIS PLAGUING WIND-SURFERS

The headline described the state of the Mediterranean around Barcelona during training for the 1992 Olympics. Not only rats, but used condoms and refrigerators, competed with the wind-surfing athletes practising for the upcoming competition.

—from the *Calgary Herald*, July 15, 1992

FACING PAGE: *Photograph by Stephen Dalton/NHPA.*

Roumania

A newspaper article by Victoria Clark describes the state of the rat population in Bucharest, where it is officially estimated that there is at least one rat per person—about 2 million. Unofficial estimates guess at possibly five rats per person, helping to explain the sensation that rats are everywhere, "caught in the beam of a car's headlights, scuttling into the hole next to the elevator and into the overflowing garbage cans behind the apartment blocks."—from Victoria Clark, *London Observer*, reprinted in *Montreal Gazette*, November 16, 1992

Spain

In La Granja every room that was not in use had been turned into a latrine—a frightful shambles of smashed furniture and excrement . . . In the great courtyard where the cooks ladled out the rations the litter of rusty tins, mud, mule dung, and decaying food was revolting. It gave point to the old army song:

There are rats, rats,
Rats as big as cats,
In the quartermaster's store!

The ones at La Granja itself really were as big as cats, or nearly; great bloated brutes that waddled over the beds of mulch, too impudent even to run away unless you shot at them.—George Orwell, *Homage to Catalonia*, 78

Turkey

They stepped inside. Another few yards' climb, Bond thought, and mass hysteria must have seized the distant thousands of rats further up the tunnel. The horde would have turned. Out of sheer pressure for space, the rats would have braved the lights and hurled themselves down on to the two intruders, in spite of the two glaring eyes and threatening scent.

"Watch," said Kerim.

There was a moment of silence. Further up the tunnel the squeaking had stopped, as if at a word of command. Then suddenly the tunnel was

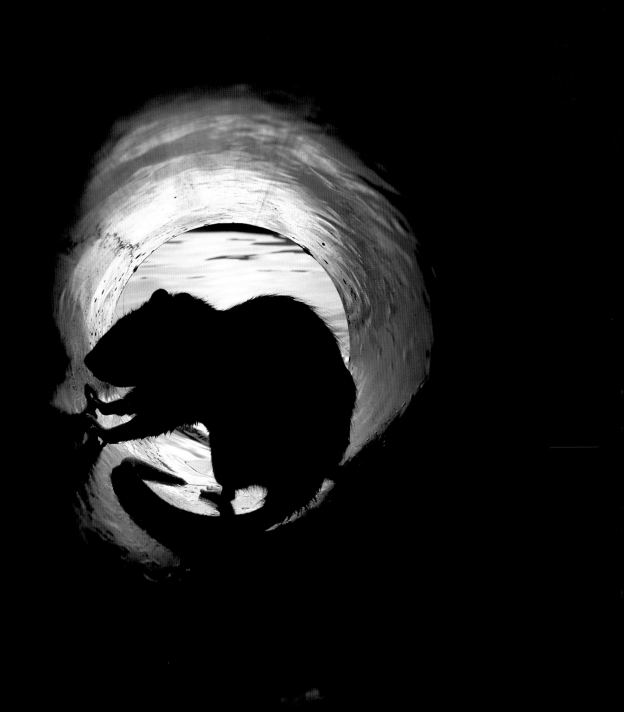

MAN KEPT PET RATS

According to the *Province*, Angelo Russo, 76 years old and a resident of Deltona, was taken for a psychiatric examination after it was discovered that he had over 230 rats in his home. The rats, who had lived with Russo for years, were exterminated.—from "Briefly," Vancouver *Province*, June 30, 1995

BOSTON

An article in *Time* warned of a potential rat invasion due to the reconstruction of a major freeway through Boston's centre. The rebuilding, necessitating the removal of miles of subterranean pipes and tunnels, would likely disrupt the thousands of rats believed to be living underground. "There are already more rats than people around here, and they're bigger than my dog," exclaimed Mark Iapicca, a parking lot manager who worked nearby.—from Sam Allis, *Time*, February 27, 1989

a foot deep in a great wave of hurling, scrambling grey bodies as, with a continuous high-pitched squeal, the rats turned and pelted back down the slope . . .

Kerim gave a non-committal grunt. "One of these days those rats will start dying. Then we shall have the plague in Istanbul again. Sometimes I feel guilty for not telling the authorities of this tunnel so they can clean the place up. But I can't so long as the Russians are up here."—Ian Fleming, *From Russia with Love*, 116

United States

New York

As a rule, New York rats are nocturnal. They rove in the streets in many neighborhoods, but only after the sun has set. They steal along as quietly as spooks in the shadows close to the building line, or in the gutters, peering this way and that, sniffing, quivering . . . The average person rarely sees one. When he does, it is a disquieting experience. Anyone who has been confronted by a rat in the bleakness of a Manhattan dawn and has seen it whirl and slink away, its claws rasping against the pavement, thereafter understands fully why this beast has been for centuries a symbol of the Judas and the stool pigeon, of soullessness in general.—Joseph Mitchell, "The Rats on the Waterfront," 55

A practice called "airmailing" was described by Thomas Canby in his *National Geographic* article about the rat. Airmailing, or jettisoning trash from upper floors of New York apartment buildings in poorer sections of the city, occurred when the tenants of buildings were too afraid to descend to the street or to the basement to dispose of their garbage in more orthodox ways. Canby described the habit as a bonanza for rats, as it left garbage strewn about the streets.—from Thomas Y. Canby, "The Rat: Lapdog of the Devil," *National Geographic*, July 1977, 78–79

Virginia

RATS' NESTS YIELD STORE OF TINY DOMESTIC TREASURES

"It's so exciting," curator Susan Borchardt said. "We love rats' nests."

Archaeologists and historians have another source for clues to the past. A search through an eighteenth-century home in Mason Neck revealed that the odds and ends collected by industrious rats provide valuable information about clothing, wallpapers, newspapers and household objects. Restorer Charles Phillips has frequently used the scraps found in these antique nests to help him in his restoration of house interiors, and a New York fabric firm now sells reproductions of a cloth found in a nest in a colonial cottage in Williamsburg. —from Stephen Kreider Yoder, *Wall Street Journal*, March 25, 1995

Washington, D.C.

Mr Winn of the Washington, D.C., public health department related a number of rat encounters his division has experienced, including a frantic call from a woman who found a rat in a toilet bowl in a building on Capitol Hill. "People are particularly conscious about something coming up the commode," he said.

At another location, close to trash dumpsters and blackberry bushes, five to six hundred rat burrows were discovered. The rats were dining without effort and their numbers were increasing rapidly as a result.

One very disturbing incident involved a sleeping baby bitten by rats. This occurred in a badly infested apartment where rat holes could be found along every baseboard.

"Rats are like people, they buy a home that's convenient to everything— like shopping centres, food sources, dumpsters."—interview by Barbara Smith with Mr Winn, Department of Public Health, Washington, D.C.

LOS ANGELES

The palm trees that grace the streets of Los Angeles, all planted by man's beautifying hand, none native, are home to thousands of rats' nests. At times a rat, or two, will fall from the top of a bushy-headed palm into a passing convertible car, altering the consciousness of the driver.—David Homel, *Rat Palms*, epigraph

OF ALL THOSE RATS IN WASHINGTON, D.C., MOST ARE RODENTS

—headline from the *Wall Street Journal*, November 24, 1992

VIETNAM

HANOI'S METROPOLE HOTEL KICKS OUT THE RATS

A major renovation at the Metropole, built in 1911, has given the heave to the one-time main entertainment— "rat chasing." The hotel has reopened as a luxury, four-star hotel with, hopefully, not a rat in sight.—from Kathleen Callo, Reuters, November 28, 1992

3. THE ESSENTIAL RAT

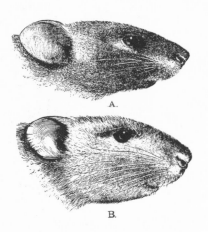

ABOVE: *Illustrations of the black rat and brown rat from the ninth edition of the* Encyclopædia Britannica, *1878.*

FACING PAGE: *Eighteenth-century engraving from a drawing by Buffon (Georges-Louis Leclerc, comte de Buffon) of "Le Surmulot," the brown rat, c. 1756.*

A quick perusal of the rat literature reveals a confusing variety of names for rats. Humankind generally concerns itself with the two main varieties: the black rat and the brown rat. The black rat, the carrier of the bubonic plague bacillus, is commonly believed to have arrived in Europe in the twelfth century from Asia. The brown rat is believed to have arrived in Europe, again from Asia, during the early eighteenth century. Specific dates have been recorded by J.F.D. Shrewsbury in his book, *A History of the Bubonic Plague,* for the brown rat's arrival: first appearance in Britain, 1728; in France, 1750; in Norway, 1764; in the U.S., 1775; in Switzerland, 1809; and in Spain, 1880. An amusing comment in Arnold Mallis's *Handbook on Pest Control* questions the reliability of the dates of these sightings: "Did they carry passports?" he asks. But others argue that rats have been in Europe as long as people, if not longer. According to both Shrewsbury and Mallis, there are Pliocene remains in Lombardy, Quaternary remains near Pisa, Pleistocene remains in Crete, and a multitude of references in Greek and Roman literature. Shrewsbury discusses the possibility that the rat became extinct in Europe and was reintroduced. It can't be denied that plague has long existed, long before the first great pandemic of the 1100s. There are references to bubonic plague in the Levant around 300 B.C. and the Bible also refers to plague in 1 Samuel 6:4. As well, an early indication of rats in the British Isles comes from an illustration in *The Book of Kells,* Matthew 1, 18: (folio 34r), which was produced between the sixth and ninth centuries. A good reproduction can be found in Bernard Meehan's edition.

Some of the confusion is due to the lack of distinction in names for mice and rats. The generic name *mus,* used to identify both rats and mice, was replaced in 1910 by the word *rattus.* The brown rat, known up to that time as *Mus deca-manus,* became *Rattus norvegicus.* The black rat, *Mus rattus,* became *Rattus rattus.*

LE SURMULOT.

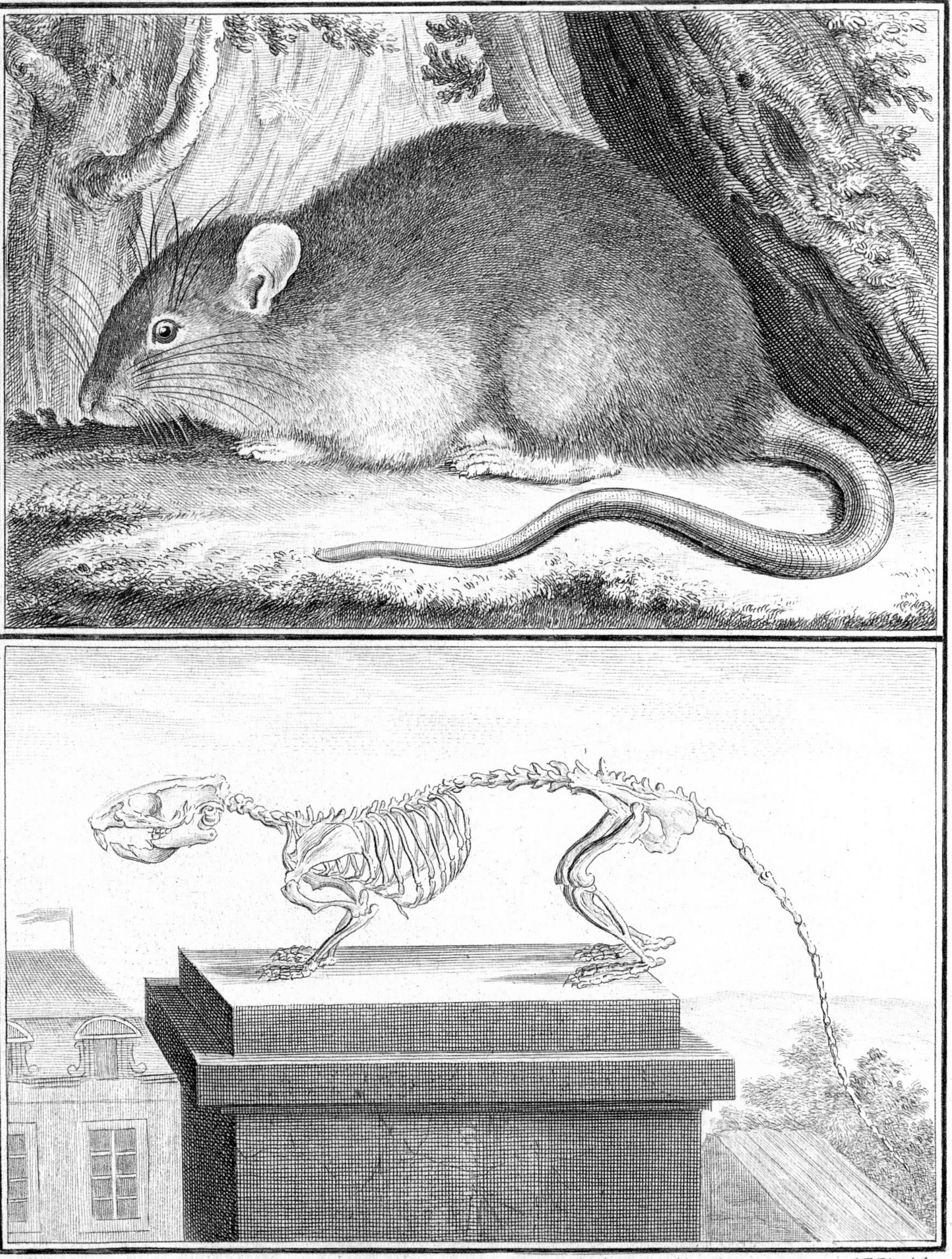

Rattus norvegicus

ALSO KNOWN AS:

MUS DECAMANUS

NORWAY RAT

BROWN RAT

COMMON RAT

GREY RAT

WHARF RAT

WATER-RAT

BARN RAT

FIELD RAT

SEWER RAT

MIGRATORY RAT

HANOVERIAN RAT*

*Called this by the British, who thought that it came from Germany and that naturally nothing good could come from there.

Where the brown rat lives no other rat may survive. They are xenophobes and patriots from Chinese Mongolia. They can gnaw through wood, concrete, and steel. They attack and kill members of their own species. They wage intertribal war. They kill the female of the species and their own young. They are cannibals. They cannot vomit and so can eat almost anything. They are almost totally blind and "see" with the hairs on the sides of their bodies. They migrate often, bringing with them plague and devastation. They will gnaw off their own legs to get out of a trap. They are utterly destructive of all other forms of life.—Gilbert Sorrentino, *Splendide-Hôtel*, 30

Two examples of counterfeit rats: the cotton rat (left) *and the hedgehog rat* (right), *both from the* Century Encyclopædia

FACING PAGE: Rattus norvegicus (le surmulot *or the brown rat*)

THIS PAGE: Rattus rattus (le rat domestique *or the black rat*) *from* Porte-feuille des enfans, *Vol. 2, by Charles Frederic, 1795*

RAT FACTS

LITTER SIZE:	Norway rat: 6–22 pups, average 7–8
	Black rat: 6–8
SEXUAL MATURITY:	Norway rat: after 2 months
	Black rat: after 4 months
GESTATION:	21–25 days
ACHIEVEMENTS:	A *Rattus rattus* can jump as high as four feet.

Rattus rattus

ALSO KNOWN AS:

MUS RATTUS
BLACK RAT
SHIP RAT
ROOF RAT
HOUSE RAT
PLAGUE RAT

The U.S. Department of Agriculture has decided that rats, mice and birds do not qualify as animals. They were given this freedom of definition by a 1971 revision of the Animal Welfare Act, an act that concerns animals used in medical research. This means that there are vitually no rules governing the care and use of these popular laboratory subjects. Attempts to change this exemption have been successfully appealed by the USDA.—from Rick Weiss, *Washington Post*, July 5, 1994

Brown rats have contributed to the near-extinction of the Lord Howe white eye and Lord Howe thrush. Photograph by Rosamond Wolff Purcell

In fact, [the rat] has conquered the world. Only the extreme cold of Greenland does not seem to attract it. Unlike the Eskimo, it has had the good sense, whenever introduced to the Arctic regions, to wander southward at the first opportunity.—Hans Zinsser, *Rats, Lice and History*, 201–2

Descriptions of rats generally include a number of superlatives: they breed the most, they eat the most, they destroy the most. One remarkable thing about rats, and about other rodents, is that their incisors never stop growing from the base out, so they need to wear down the tips in order to keep them under control. If they didn't gnaw continually, their incisors would grow 4 inches a year and cause the animal great difficulties. So gnaw they do, on concrete, insulation, wires, steel—anything we put in their way.

The rat also has a phenomenal ability to reproduce in great numbers:

"The male'll screw any female irrespective," the King said impatiently, "and there ain't no season."

"Just like us, you mean?" Jones said agreeably.

"Yes. I suppose so," said Peter Marlowe. "Anyway, the male rat will mate at any season and the female can have up to twelve litters per year, around twelve per litter, but perhaps as many as fourteen. The young are born blind and helpless twenty-two days after—contact." He picked the word delicately. "The young open their eyes after fourteen to seventeen days and become sexually mature in two months. They cease breeding at about two years and are old at three years."

"Holy cow!" Max said delightedly in the awed silence. "We sure as hell've problems. Why, if the young'll breed in two months, and we get twelve—say for round figures ten a litter—figure it for yourself. Say we get ten young on Day One. Another ten on Day Thirty. By Day Sixty the first five pair've bred, and we get fifty. Day Ninety we got another five pairs breeding and another fifty. Day One-twenty, we got two-fifty plus another fifty and another fifty and a new batch of two-fifty. For Chrissake, that makes six-fifty in five months. The next month we got near six thousand five hundred—"

"Jesus, we got us a gold mine!"—James Clavell, *King Rat*, 106

The Rats

Scales of rat-justice, rat-precision,
Libraries recording rat-right and rat-wrong
Rats that nip away each toe
And suck the soles of too thin feet
Rats that eat your eyes like oysters
Spread false trails over burrowed hills
Swamp-rats wood-rats tree-rats
Plague-rats, pet-rats army and police-rats
Sadist-rats that will not kill
Kind rats that drug you in the night
Rats that let you crush them in the garden
—Alan Sillitoe, *The Rats and Other Poems*, 31

"A dog is a mammal."

"So's a rat," Denise said.

"A rat is a vermin," Babette said.

"Mostly what a rat is," Heinrich said, "is a rodent."

"It's also a vermin."

"A cockroach is a vermin," Steffie said.

"A cockroach is an insect. You count the legs is how you know."

"It's also a vermin."

"Does a cockroach get cancer? No," Denise said. "That means a rat is more like a human than it is like a cockroach, even if they're both vermins, since a rat and a human can get cancer but a cockroach can't."—Don Delillo, *White Noise*, 124

References to mice, and possibly rats, in the Bible (Leviticus 11:29 and Isaiah 66:17) define the *mus* as a forbidden food:
These also shall be unclean unto you among the creeping things that creep upon the earth; the weasel, and the mouse, and the tortoise after his kind.—Leviticus 11:29

An urban coyote can eat one rat per hour.—Robert Mason Lee, *Globe and Mail*, February 3, 1996

4. THE FABLED RAT

*Translation:

THE FABLE OF THE RAT AND THE FROG
As a rat went in pilgrimage, he came by a river, and demanded help of a frog for to pass and go over the water. And then the frog bound the rat's foot to her foot, and thus swam unto the middle of the river. And as they were there the frog stood still, to the end that the rat should be drowned. And in the meanwhile came a kite upon them and bare them both with him.

He that thinketh evil against good, the evil that he thinketh shall fall upon himself.—John J. McKendry, *Aesop: Five Centuries of Illustrated Fables,* 24

Few animals have been as badly treated in fable as the rat. For example, *Aesop's Fables* resulted from the confusion regarding the Greek word *mus* (the early Greeks made as little distinction between rats and mice as they did between foreigners, labelling all rats and mice *mus* and all foreigners *barbarians*). The result of using the generic word, which later came to mean specifically mouse, was that most translations of Aesop's fables distinguish the mouse as the star and neglect the rat. Satisfying as this might be to those too squeamish to tolerate a rat in their fables, it provokes a certain distrust of the illustrations that accompany most translations. The "mice" shown are generally depicted as larger than the average house cat and cunningly endowed with many ratty features.

William Caxton's interpretation of *Aesop's Fables* should have cleared up the confusion, especially since it was produced around 1484, so long ago. He very specifically grants the rat first place wherever it deserves it. The problem with Caxton is that he wrote in Old English, and who's going to read that nowadays?

The thyrd fable is of the rat/ and of the frogge/*
Now it be so/ that as the rat wente in pylgremage/ he came by a Ryuer/ and demaunded helpe of a frogge for to passe/ and go ouer the water/ And thenne the frogge bound the rats foote to her foote/ and thus swymed vnto the myddes ouer the Ryuer/ And as they were there the frogge stood stylle/ to thende that the rat shold be drowned/ And in the meane whyle came a kyte vpon them/ and bothe bare them with hym/ This fable made Esope for a symylytude whiche is prouffitable to many folkes/ For he that thynketh euylle ageynst good/ the euylle whiche he thynketh shall ones falle vpon hym self—R. T. Lenaghan, *Caxton's Aesop,* 76

Fifteenth-century woodcuts by William Caxton illustrating "The Rat, the Frog, and the Kite" (left) from Aesopo Hisoriado, *1497, and "The Cat and the Rat" (above) from the* Fabulos de Esopo, *1489.*

ANCIENT MYTHS

Specific references to rats in ancient literature are nonexistent, as the Greek word *mus* was used universally to describe mice and rats without distinction between the two mouselike rodents, and so we see references to mice but not rats in Herodotus, the myths and early histories. Aelian, mentioned in Arnold Mallis's *Handbook on Pest Control*, wrote in the second century A.D. that " 'Caspian rats' at times migrate in countless hosts and bridge the rivers, forming live rafts, each rat holding by teeth to the tail of the rat in front." But the word *rat* here was used at the discretion of the translator.

The god Apollo, Apollo Smintheus, has been variously described as the Rat-Apollo and the Mouse-Apollo. Robert Graves explains the connection between Apollo and rodents:

One component in Apollo's godhead seems to have been an oracular mouse—Apollo Smintheus ("Mouse-Apollo") is among his earliest titles . . . Mice were associated with disease and its cure, and the Hellenes therefore worshipped Apollo as a god of medicine and prophecy.—Robert Graves, *The Greek Myths*, Vol. 1, 56–57

Herodotus, in his description of the battle between the Egyptians and the Assyrians, describes a plague of rodents and calls the animals mice, but from the description of gnawing and swarming, they could easily have been rats:

[The Egyptian king Sethos] marched to Pelusium, which guards the approaches to Egypt, and there took up his position. As he lay here facing the Assyrians, thousands of field-mice swarmed over them during the night, and ate their quivers, their bowstrings, and the leather handles of their shields, so that on the following day, having no arms to fight with, they abandoned their position and suffered severe losses during their retreat. There is still a stone statue of Sethos in the temple of Hephaestus; the figure is represented with a mouse in its hand, and the inscription: "Look upon me and learn reverence."—Herodotus, *The Histories*, 158

FABLES

Although *Aesop's Fables* recount many tales involving mice, Jean de la Fontaine (1621–1695), the great French fabulist, deferred to the rat in his fables. He drew on the works of Aesop, the Bible, the Indian fables of Bidpaï and his own fertile imagination. His twelve books of fables were published between 1668 and 1694 and have been frequently republished in collected editions, adorned with the images of such artists as J. J. Grandville and Gustave Doré.

As with most fables, the object is to tell a story with a moral. In the fable "The City Rat and the Country Rat," translated by Elizur Wright in 1842, the city rat invites his country friend to dine with him on turtle soup in sumptuous surroundings. They are rudely interrupted and frightened off. The country rat declines the city rat's offer to return to the meal, saying,

> To-morrow dine with me.
> I'm not offended at
>   Your feast so grand and free,—
>
> For I've no fare resembling;
>   But then I eat at leisure,
>   And would not swap, for pleasure
> So mix'd with fear and trembling.

"The Lion and the Rat" tells the story of the lion who, once having spared the life of a rat, is saved from a trap by that same rat. "The Cat and the Old Rat" relates the tale of the crafty cat known as "the Attila, the scourge of rats," who contrives to hang himself upside-down and play dead in the granary in order to trick the rats into coming out into the open. The ploy works: the rats are overjoyed to think the crafty cat got his comeuppance, and they come out to celebrate his death. The cat releases himself from his gallows and tears into the rats, destroying them left and right, until spotted by a wary old battleworn rat.

The rats of Pontus, which be only white, . . . some say, when the male or female is laden with grass and herbs . . . it lieth upon the back with the said provision upon their bellies, and then cometh the other, and taketh hold by the tail with the mouth, and draweth the fellow into the earth: thus do they one by the other in turns: and hereupon it is, that all that time their backs are bare, and the hair worn off.—Pliny, *Pliny's Natural History,* 96

BELOW: *J. J. Grandville's illustration for la Fontaine's fable "The Two Rats, the Fox, and the Egg" clearly depicts the legend also told by Pliny, above.*
LEFT: *The J. Desandré illustration for "The City Rat and the Country Rat."*

Other rat fables of la Fontaine include:

"The Frog and the Rat"

"The Hermit Rat"

"The Rat and the Oyster"

"The Rat and the Elephant"

"The Cat and the Rat"

"The Raven, the Gazelle, the Tortoise
    and the Rat"

"The Lion and the Rat"

"Council Held by the Rats"

"The Weasel in the Granary"

"The War of the Rats and the Weasels"

Most readers will recollect the fable, where a young mouse suggests that the cat should have a bell fastened to his neck, so that his companions might be aware of her approach . . . This experiment has actually been tried upon a rat. A bell was fastened round his neck, and he was replaced in his hole, with full expectation of his frightening the rest away; but it turned out that, instead of their continuing to be alarmed at his approach, he was heard for the space of a year to frolic and scamper with them.—*Chambers Book of Days*, Vol. 2, 104

FACING PAGE: *Gustave Doré's illustration for the la Fontaine fable "The Cat and the Old Rat."*

J.J. Grandville's illustration of la Fontaine's fable "The League of Rats."

Most of the tales have much to do with adversarial confrontations and all are concerned with survival in one way or another.

Similar tales are found in the literature of India and the Near East. The fabulously illustrated fables of Bidpaï and a counterpart from the fifteenth century Mongol Court, *Kalila Wa Dimna*, present a number of rodent fables, including "The Cat in the Trap," "The Rat, the Weasel, and the Owl in the Tree," "The Ascetic and the Adopted Mouse (or Rat)" and "The Frightened Mouse (Rat) and the Trapped Cat." Depending on the translator, the rodents will be either mice or rats. In all of the illustrations, the mice are large enough to be killer rats. Beautiful renditions of these tales can be found in Jill Sanchia Cowan's book *Kalila Wa Dimna* and in Ernst J. Grube's book *A Mirror for Princes from India*.

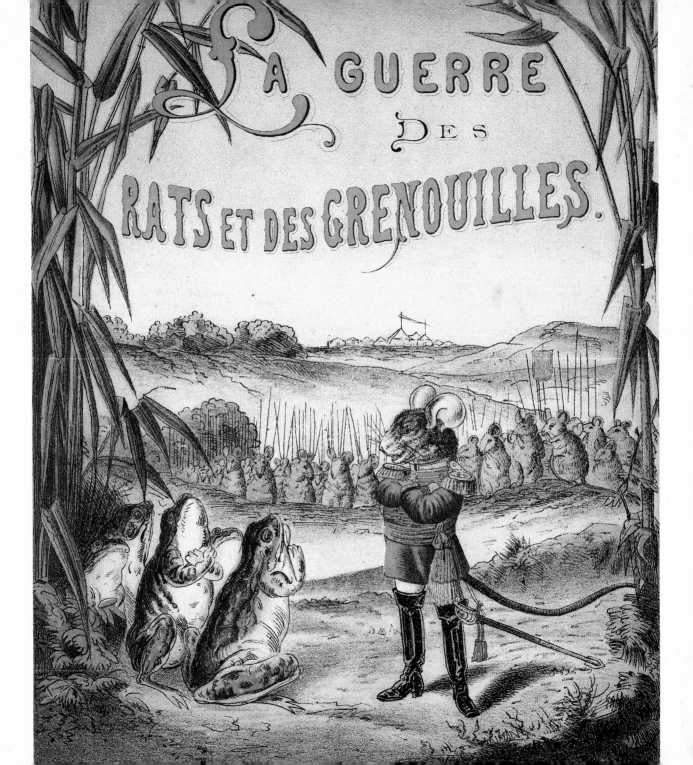

La Guerre des rats et des grenouilles (*The War of the Rats and the Frogs*) is a delightful children's book from the turn of the century. Inspired by la Fontaine's tale of the battle of the rats and the weasels, it tells the story of the death of Psicarpax, the son of Ratapon, the king of the rats. Ratapon swears to avenge the death of his son and rallies the rat troops to fight against the frogs. The illustration on the facing page shows the cover; the one on the left shows two rats recovering from injuries received during one of the several battles, and the one on the right shows a battle in progress with the frogs getting the short end of the stick.

ABOVE: *Gustave Doré illustration of the la Fontaine fable "Le rat et le chat" ("The Cat and the Rat").*

RIGHT: *Doré illustration of "Le rat et l'éléphant" ("The Rat and the Elephant").*

FAR RIGHT: *Australian brown-footed rat* (Mus fuscipes) *from the* Encyclopædia Britannica, *ninth edition, 1878.*

Desandré illustration of "Le rat et l'éléphant" ("The Rat and the Elephant").

Fables about rats exist around the world. The Chinese have chosen the rat as the number one animal in their pantheon of astrological animals; rats are considered a sign of prosperity in Japan; and the rat is the object of worship at the temple of Deshnoke in India. On the plus side, the rat has been used as a talisman, a sign of spirits and an effective medicinal cure; on the negative side, it has been considered bad luck and a sign of evil. Here is a sampling of rat fable and myth from a number of countries.

Australia

Simple and effectual is the expedient adopted by natives of Central Australia who desire to cultivate their beards. They prick the chin all over with a pointed bone, and then stroke it carefully with a magic stick or stone, which represents a kind of rat that has very long whiskers. The virtue of these whiskers naturally passes into the representative stick or stone, and thence by an easy transition to the chin, which, consequently, is soon adorned with a rich growth of beard.—James George Frazer, *The Golden Bough*, 32

Burma

And even beyond his grave his success would continue. According to Buddhist belief, those who have done evil in their lives will spend the next incarnation in the shape of a rat, a frog or some other low animal. U Po Kyin was a good Buddhist and intended to provide against this danger. He would devote his closing years to good works, which would pile up enough merit to outweigh the rest of his life . . . And he would return to the earth in male human shape—for a woman ranks at about the same level as a rat or a frog—or at worst as some dignified beast such as an elephant.—George Orwell, *Burmese Days*, 7–8

Tegearek at last decided, with the assistance of Asok-meke, that the failure of the piglets was a consequence of eating rats. Rats were not bad for pigs, which hunt out and eat with relish almost anything, but the ghosts of their rodent victims had banded together in revenge against the pigs and conspired against the piglets' growth. To warn the rat ghosts that he is on to them, and to banish their influence from Patosaki, Tegearek had erected these two poles.—Peter Matthiessen, *Under the Mountain Wall*, 198

China Chinese Astrology

The rat has a place of great importance in Chinese mythology, being the first of twelve animals in the Chinese zodiac. It is believed that the year of the Rat is a year of prosperity and hard work.

I have found several stories that relate why the rat was given the distinction of being the first animal in the Chinese zodiac—both involve intelligence and both explain that the ox had originally been given the number one spot. The first version, related by Wolfram Eberhard in *A Dictionary of Chinese Symbols*, tells the story of the animals who wanted to be considered for the zodiac lining up. The ox was first in line and unbeknownst to either the ox or to the others in line, a rat had hitched a ride on the ox's back. When it came time to choose the animals, the rat jumped off and was picked first.

Eberhard also tells the second version, in which the rat and the ox quarrel about who is bigger. The ox is astounded that the rat has the nerve to claim the distinction and tells him so:

"Everyone knows that I, the ox, am big and immeasurably strong. How can a rat that only weighs a few pounds dare to compete with me? I call it ridiculous."

Nineteenth-century hand-coloured engraving from England, depicting a black rat (Mus Rattus).

CHINA
Some astrological facts:
The rat rules from 11 P.M. until 1 A.M.
The rat's season is winter
The rat sign corresponds to Sagittarius
The year of the Rat takes place every twelve years: 1996, 2008, 2020 and so on.

—from Theodora Lau, *Handbook of Chinese Horoscopes*

It seems that in Newfoundland, threats are a common way to exhort children to behave well. A study group found that of 1870 threats recorded, 132 referred to animals. The rat placed high on the list, just after the bear:

bear	30
rat	26
(fish, big fish)	12
dog	9
moose	6
mouse	5
shark	4

—J.R. Porter and W.M.S. Russell, *Animals in Folklore*, 37

Dreaming of (or seeing) rats (numerous) is a sign of death.—*Heart's Content*, Newfoundland.—Fanny D. Bergen, "Dreams: Animals," 70

Rat, eighteenth century. This catch-penny illustration by Bowles and Carver was one of thousands sold for a penny a sheet on the streets of London.

The rat sneers at the ox, so they decide to walk out among the people and let them decide. But before they leave, the rat affects a sudden humility and convinces the ox that he should be allowed to increase his size a little. The ox agrees, never dreaming that his generosity will backfire. The rat doubles in size and amazes the townspeople, who exclaim, "Look! Never before have I seen such a big rat. It is incredibly big." The ox, fooled by the rat and ignored by all, had to concede his place in the zodiac.—from Wolfram Eberhard, *Folktales of China*, 186–87

Rats used to be left undisturbed on certain days of the year so that they could get married in peace! . . . In a South Chinese legend, it is the rat which brings rice to mankind. Rats can turn into demons—male demons usually, in contrast with the fox which turns into a female demon . . .

There is frequent mention in early texts of rat-dance in which the rats stand up on their hind legs, place their front paws on their heads and sing.
—Wolfram Eberhard, *A Dictionary of Chinese Symbols*, 246–47

On the last day of the old year, rats are said to be running here, there, and everywhere, seeking their mates, and availing themselves of such a good opportunity for eavesdropping. If they hear nothing said about them in a house . . . they will not trouble themselves to go to that house again. But if, unfortunately, the word *rat* is mentioned in their hearing, they will be sure to return in great force on the following year, causing great discomfort to the inhabitants.—M.T. Mansfield, "Chinese Superstition," *The Folk-lore Journal*, 129

Germany Bishop Hatto

This legend tells the story of a greedy cleric, Bishop Hatto, living off the fat of the land during the famine of 970 while people around him starved to death. Fed up with the whining of the starving, he locked them into a barn and set it on fire. He then went home, ate a huge supper and slept that night like a baby. But

> In the morning as he enter'd the hall
> Where his picture hung against the wall,
> A sweat like death all over him came,
> For the rats had eaten it out of the frame.

His servants panicked and reported that scores of rats were marching towards his castle, devouring everything in their way and blackening the fields with the numbers of their bodies. Bishop Hatto escaped to a tower he owned called the Mäusthurm, or Mouse Tower, on an island in the Rhine, but the rats swam over, climbed up and around the tower, and Bishop Hatto met his maker:

> They have whetted their teeth against the stones,
> And now they pick the Bishop's bones;
> They gnawed the flesh from every limb,
> For they were sent to do judgment on him.

Similar catastrophes are said to have happened to other bishops, and there are other mouse towers and mouse castles in Germany. The myth-historian Sabine Baring-Gould believed that these stories grew from the Teutonic tradition of human sacrifice during times of famine: similar incidents were recorded in the thirteenth century in Sweden and Denmark, and rats and mice were considered as sacred animals and as souls of the dead. From this, he concluded that the death of Hatto was possibly a sacrifice, but that later when the practice was discontinued, his death was interpreted as a judgement of God.—from Sabine Baring-Gould, "Bishop Hatto," in *Curious Myths of the Middle Ages*, 123–26

GERMANY

It is a bad omen if rats leave a house for no apparent reason. Either the building is unsound and likely to fall, or some dire misfortune threatens someone living within. If they gnaw the hangings of a room, there will be a death in the family before long.—E. and M.A. Radford, *Encyclopaedia of Superstitions*, 280

Gustave Doré's illustration for Puss in Boots, *a fairy tale by Charles Perrault (1628–1703).*

Nineteenth-century hand-coloured engraving from France.

Germany The Pied Piper

> Rats!
> They fought the dogs and killed the cats,
>   And bit the babies in the cradles,
> And ate the cheeses out of the vats,
>   And licked the soup from the cooks' own ladles,
> Split open the kegs of salted sprats,
> Made nests inside men's Sunday hats,
> And even spoiled the women's chats
>   By drowning their speaking
>   With shrieking and squeaking
> In fifty different sharps and flats.
> —Robert Browning, "The Pied Piper of Hamelin"

Sabine Baring-Gould also relates the tale of the Pied Piper of Hamelin, probably the most famous rat fable in existence. A number of variations of the tale exist, but most essential facts are shared by all of the tales. *Chambers Book of Days* claims that the tale took place on July 22, 1376, but most other sources place it as occurring on June 26, 1284. The Pied Piper is the story of the people of the town of Hamelin (Hameln) who, fed up with the damage done to their granaries by rats, hired a piper to lure the rats away. A sum was agreed upon and the piper did his job, but the townspeople decided to cheat him of his fee. In retaliation:

> He threatened them with revenge; they bade him do his worst, whereupon he betakes him again to his pipe, and going through the streets as before, was followed by a number of boys out of one of the gates of the city, and coming to a little hill, there opened in the side thereof a wide hole, into the which himself and all the children did enter; and being entered, the hill did close up again, and became as before. A boy, that, being lame, came somewhat lagging behind the rest, seeing this that happened, returned

English catchpenny illustration, nineteenth century.

Monkey and Rat

presently back, and told what he had seen; forthwith began great lamentation among the parents for their children, and the men were sent out with all diligence, both by land and by water, to inquire if aught could be heard of them; but with all the inquiry they could possibly use, nothing more than is aforesaid could of them be understood. And this great wonder happened on the 22d day of July, in the year of our Lord 1376.
—*Chambers Book of Days*, Vol. 2, 103

One of Mr Bewick's rat illustrations.

Günter Grass, in his novel *The Rat*, offers a new explanation for why the village called in the Pied Piper. He took into consideration the lack of historical evidence that a large group of children had ever disappeared at that time or that rat catchers had ever played flutes to attract their intended victims. The possibility that the children leaving represented a children's crusade has been raised by others, but Grass also swept away that idea. He declared that the children had taken to carrying rats about in order to annoy their parents. The older folk, in retaliation, hired a piper to come into the town on Saint John's Day and lure them to an outing in a cave in Mount Calvary, close by. One hundred and thirty children and their rats were given a big party complete with sausages and beer:

The singing, it seems, was hellish.

But when the party was at its height and the barley beer had steeped the children in lethargy, the piper crept out of the cave. Then the entrance, as wide as a barn door, was sealed by the town constable, walled in by masons, covered over with carloads of sand by peasants, and sprinkled mercilessly with holy water by priests. It appears that not much screaming was heard from the cave. Rumors that circulated later spoke of a single escaped rat.—Günter Grass, *The Rat*, 301–2

GREAT BRITAIN

Mr Bewick, the ingenious wood-engraver, has put on record a fact regarding rats nearly as mystical as any of the above. He alleges that "the skins of such of them as have been devoured in their holes [for they are cannibals to a sad extent] have frequently been found curiously turned inside out, every part of them being completely inverted, even to the ends of the toes."—*Chambers Book of Days*, Vol. 2, 103

Rats are used in threats to encourage obedience and good behaviour, ("I've got rats stored up in my attic for naughty little boys like you"), to keep children out of the cellar and dark, dangerous or forbidden places, to get them to bed and to sleep, and to discourage them from eating food in bed.—J. R. Porter and W.M.S. Russell, *Animals in Folklore*, 39

JAMAICA

Puppy nyam ratta done, him cut capers 'pon John-crow.

When the pup has eaten a rat, he chases the crows; applied to one who has food given him and goes away without thanks.—Martha Warren Beckwith, *Jamaica Folk-lore*, 98

JAPAN

The Seven Gods of Good Luck (*Shichi Fukujin*), so conspicuous in the various phases of Japanese art, can endow one with fame, love, talents, riches, sustenance, contentment, and longevity. Two of them, the whimsical *Daikoku* (son of *Susano-o*), the God of Wealth; and *Ebisu*, the God of Sustenance, and protector of the fisherman, are to be found in almost every house. The former occupies an honored place on certain of the paper money, and he is usually represented sitting or standing on bags of rice, which rats come to gnaw at under his indulgent eyes.

—Philip T. Terry, *Terry's Guide to the Japanese Empire*, ccviii

Ireland

This Irish folktale tells of a gifted sailor who was able to banish rats, in retaliation for the destruction of a prized suit:

[The sailor] took out his razor and laid it edge upward on the deck. The razor was not long on the deck when out came a rat, rubbed its mouth along the edge of the razor and kissed it. Then it ran back to where it had come from. Other rats followed, one by one; each of them rubbed its mouth along the edge of the razor, kissing it, and then ran away again. After a few score of them had done that, there finally came out a rat, screaming loudly. She went up to the razor and rubbed her neck along its edge, until she fell dead beside it.

The captain of the ship had been watching what was going on from the first rat to the last, which had cut its throat on the razor. He . . . called the sailor to him . . . and ordered him to leave the ship.

"You could have done that trick to any man on board," said he, "as easily as you did it to the rat."—Sean O'Sullivan, *Folktales of Ireland*, 223

According to O'Sullivan, this story of the sailor illustrated the Irish belief that charmed individuals who wrote a poem on a piece of paper and then left it at a place where it was known the rats lived could get rid of them. If the charm worked, then the leader of the rats would emerge carrying the poem and the rats would depart to a location described on the piece of paper. This was a useful means not only of getting rid of rats but of getting back at someone else.

Morocco

Dried rats can still be found hanging in Moroccan apothecary shops in the old markets of cities such as Fez and Casablanca. They keep company with live tortoises and dead birds and reptiles. The sight of these garlands of desiccated animals is both compelling and revolting.

The reason was there are no rats at Bäb Ftöh, one of the city gates of Fez, is that once a saint belonging to the family of the Fäsîyin stuck a knife into the ground with a charm written on it, the baraka [blessedness] of which attracted all the rats of the neighbourhood, with the result that the knife cut off their heads.—Edward Westermarck, *Ritual and Belief in Morocco*, 210

North America An Urban Legend

I first heard the following story around 1985 from a friend who had heard it from her hairdresser, who swore she heard it directly from one of her clients:

A family drove down from Canada to Mexico for a vacation at a small beach resort. While there, one of the children noticed a scrawny dog following them as they walked through the streets of the town. Attempts to chase it away were fruitless, and the family ended up adopting it. They smuggled it into their hotel room and fed it scraps brought back from restaurants. When it came time to drive back through the Mexico / U.S. border, the dog, which was as tiny as a Chihuahua, was easily hidden under a jacket, and the car was waved through. Once back in Canada, the family and the dog adjusted well to living together. The children were happy to have a new pet and the parents were pleased that their new acquisition proved itself loyal and compatible.

The day came when they realized they had to get shots for the dog, so they made an appointment with the vet. The vet looked at the dog for some time without saying a word. Then he looked at the father who had brought the dog in. "Where did you get him from?" the vet asked. "Found him in Mexico," was the father's reply. "Have you noticed anything unusual about him?" the doctor persisted. "No, nothing at all," said the father. "Why? Is there something the matter with him?" "I'll say," said the vet. "This isn't a dog, it's a rat!"

A year or so later, I found a similar story recounted in *The Mexican Pet* by Jan Harold Brunvand. I had wanted to believe it, and so had others, I suppose. The "Earthweek" column in the *Vancouver Sun* fell into the same trap by reporting a variation from Kiev's *Vseukrainskiye Vedomosti* newspaper. In this instance a Pakistani rat had been mistaken for a bull-terrier. Same myth, different locale.

IOWA

When three people are sleeping in a bed, the one next to the wall gets the wish, the one in the middle a golden slipper, and the one on the outside is for the rats and the mice.—Earl J. Stout, *Folklore from Iowa*, 161

LOUISIANA

In French Louisiana rat tails have been put into amulets or hoodoo bags along with other delectable items such as cat hairs, dried vulture or snake skin, fingernail scrapings, weeds, snake fangs, dead flies and so on. The bags are used for malevolent purposes—to bring bad luck to the intended victim.

—Elizabeth Brandon, "Folk Medicine in French Louisiana," *American Folk Medicine*

Rat illustration by the Mexican artist José Guadalupe Posada.

SOUTH AFRICA

A South African warrior who twists tufts of rats' hair among his own curly black locks will have just as many chances of avoiding the enemy's spear as the nimble rat has of avoiding things thrown at it; hence in these regions rats' hair is in great demand when war is expected.—James George Frazer, *The Golden Bough*, 31

UNITED STATES

Some years ago an American farmer was reported to have written a civil letter to the rats, telling them that his crops were short, that he could not afford to keep them through the winter, that he had been very kind to them, and that for their own good he thought they had better leave him and go to some of his neighbours who had more grain. This document he pinned to a post in his barn for the rats to read.

—James George Frazer, *The Golden Bough*, 531

Rat.

Raratonga

Far away from Europe, at Raratonga, in the Pacific, when a child's tooth was extracted, the following prayer used to be recited:

Big rat! little rat!
Here is my old tooth.
Pray give me a new one.

Then the tooth was thrown on the thatch of the house, because rats make their nests in the decayed thatch. The reason assigned for invoking the rats on these occasions was that rats' teeth were the strongest known to the natives.—James George Frazer, *The Golden Bough*, 39

Miscellaneous

J. G. Frazer wrote of the custom in many parts of the world of placing extracted teeth where they would be found by a rat or a mouse. By doing so, the owner of the tooth showed a desire to acquire the legendary strength of the rodent's tooth. He also wrote about charms for ridding farmers' fields of rats:

In the Ardennes they say that to get rid of rats you should repeat the following words: *"Erat verbum, apud Deum vestrum.* Male rats and female rats, I conjure you, by the great God, to go out of my house, out of all my habitations, and to betake yourselves to such and such a place, there to end your days. *Decretis, reversis et desembarassis virgo potens, clemens, justitiae."* Then write the same words on pieces of paper, fold them up, and place one of them under the door by which the rats are to go forth, and the other on the road which they are to take. This exorcism should be performed at sunrise.—James George Frazer, *The Golden Bough*, 531

A catchpenny rat from the eighteenth-century firm of Bowles and Carver.

RAT TRICKS

Fables and folklore recount the cleverness of rats: they know when someone has been tampering with their food, they figure out devious means of transporting awkward objects such as eggs, they dip their tails in jars to get food:

> As to oil, rats have been known to get oil out of a narrow-necked bottle in the following way:—One of them would place himself, on some convenient support, by the side of the bottle, and then, dipping his tail into the oil, would give it to another to lick. In this act there is something more than what we call instinct; there is reason and understanding.—George J. Romanes, *Animal Intelligence*, 362

Rat Kings

The term *rat king* is used to describe a bizarre phenomenon in which a number of rats—six to twenty, or thereabouts—form a circle, heads out, with their tails knotted together. The entwined group is cared for by other rats in the pack, and the animals seem to live for some time after the formation of the king. The rat king has fascinated both chroniclers and fiction writers alike, for the unexplained formation of such a grouping leads the imagination down some twisted paths.

> It is usual for kings to be put on display for some time after discovery . . . Occasionally newly discovered kings have been paraded through towns or villages so that everyone could have a good look at them. The rat king of Leipzig was kept—from 1722 onwards—in mummified form in the private museum of Dr Petermann. I often imagine the man whom I admire more than anyone else, with the possible exception of Mozart, Johann Sebastian Bach—who lived in Leipzig from 5 May 1723—going to view this particular king during a visit to Dr Petermann's museum. Unfortunately he composed no music for the occasion.—Martin Hart, *Rats*, 77

ABOVE: *Postcard from France, c. 1903. The caption reads "Ah! ça, c'est une sale blague!" ("Oh, this is a dirty trick!").*
BELOW: *Newspaper clipping along the same lines as the postcard above, 1907.*

MAUVAISE PLAISANTERIE
Le père Richaud, commissionnaire devant la gare du Nord, arrivant le matin, ouvrit sa boîte. Un rat lui sauta au visage. Richaud eut si peur qu'il mourût de cette mauvaise plaisanterie qu'on lui avait faite.

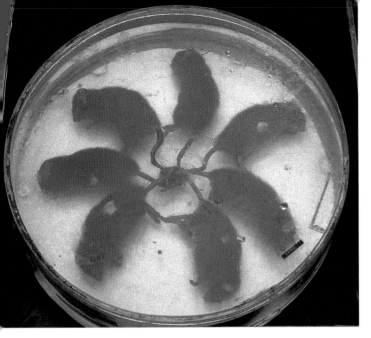

This rat king is displayed in the museum in Leiden, Holland. Photograph by Rosamond Wolff Purcell.

The famous fictional detective Aurelio Zen used the term *rat king* to describe crooked Italian politics and politicians:

"If we're all conspirators then there's no conspiracy."

"On the contrary, the condition of this conspiracy is that we're all part of it," Bartocci retorted. "It's a ratking."

"A what?"

"A ratking. Do you know what that is?"

Zen shrugged.

"The king rat, I suppose. The dominant animal in the pack."

"That's what everyone thinks. But it's not. A ratking is something that happens when too many rats live in too small a space under too much pressure. Their tails become entwined and the more they strain and stretch to free themselves the tighter grows the knot binding them, until at last it becomes a solid mass of embedded tissue . . . Not much fun, being chained to each other for life. How much sweeter it would be to run free! Nevertheless, they *do* survive, somehow. The wonders of nature, eh?"—Michael Dibdin, *Ratking*, 80–81

Eight Rats lay on the great circular bed on the dais. Three were being fed and groomed by servants. Another lay asleep. One black Rat had a secretary seated on the carpeted dais steps, reading a report to him in a low voice, and two Rats (fur so pale it was almost silver) dictated letters. The eighth Rat beckoned Desaguliers.

The Captain-General climbed the steps to kneel before the bed. The Rats lay with their bodies pointing outwards, their tails in the center of the bed's silks and pillows. Each scaly tail wound in and out of the others, tangled, tied, fixed in a fleshy knot; and Desaguliers could see (as a brown Rat page carefully cleaned) where the eight tails had inextricably grown together.—Mary Gentle, *Rats and Gargoyles*, 55

Intoxicating wheel of whirling rats, I'd rather face a dozen cats, let me out I'm going bats.—William Kotzwinkle, *Doctor Rat*, 116

48

SMART RATS

A rat who obviously didn't know how to read nevertheless loved books. So he set up house in a library where no one went any longer.

He would walk on the books, between them, run along them, contemplate them with a tear in his eye and his mouth watering. It was his home, he was happy there; these are my books, he said.

Occasionally, he'd stop to nibble at a part of one book or another.

—Phew! The new books stink of glue and ink, and their pages are flimsy and damp and stick to the palate.

Instead, he regaled himself with the most ancient pages, the dry and yellowed ones, which were very crunchy, for example his old edition of Diderot's *Encyclopedia;* he would always remember the article consecrated to God, which he made quite a feast of.

There's also a telephone book dating from 1916, full of names of dead people and obsolete addresses which he offers bites from to his buddies when they come to visit him, and which they highly prize.

His salon is furnished in paperbacks, colored and pliant. The bathroom is behind the *Letters of Madame de Sévigné.* An incunable bound in vellum whose cover is buckling serves as his bed; recently, he had a nightmare in which he was taught to read.—François Hébert, "Le rat dans la bibliothèque," *Le dernier chant de l'avant dernier dodo,* 12

We rats have . . . eaten our way to erudition . . . We are decidedly well read; in times of famine we fed on quotations; we know our belles-lettres and our philosophy inside and out; the pre-Socratics and Sophists have filled our bellies. Not to mention the Scholastics. Persistently gnawed, their involute sentences have always agreed with us.—Günter Grass, *The Rat,* 14

Gustave Doré illustration from The Fables of la Fontaine, *first published in 1868.*

The rat is the concisest tenant.
He pays not rent,—
Repudiates the obligation,
On schemes intent.

Balking our wit
To sound or circumvent,
Hate cannot harm
A foe so reticent.

Neither decree
Prohibits him,
Lawful as
Equilibrium.

—Emily Dickinson, *Selected Poems and Letters of Emily Dickinson,* 188

5. THE FICTIONAL RAT

This J.J. Grandville illustration from his book Scènes de la vie privée et publique des animaux *(1842) shows the story of the "misfortunes of rats."*

Rats appear frequently in fiction but more often than not just as scurrying shadows supplied for a hint of terror. There are few novels specifically featuring rats. Andrzej Zaniewski's novel *Rat* is an allegory describing the world from the sympathetic point of view of a rat. The novel *The Rat* by Günter Grass focuses on the gift of a rat as a means of chronicling the world's future doom. The novel *Of Rats and Diplomats* by Ahmed Ali, a political satire, describes the newly formed country of Ratistan. Children's fiction, especially books such as Robert O'Brien's *Mrs Frisby and the Rats of NIMH* and his daughter Jane Leslie Conly's sequels *Racso and the Rats of NIMH* and *R-T, Margaret, and the Rats of NIMH* treat fictional rats in a sensitive and amusing way. O'Brien's character, Nicodemus, the smartest of all children's book rats (if not all rats), speaks about his education and how his reading helped him understand the human world around him:

> Most of the books were about people; we tried to find some about rats, but there wasn't much.
>
> We did find a few things. There were two sets of encyclopedias that had sections on rats. From them we learned that we were about the most hated animals on earth, except maybe snakes and germs.
>
> That seemed strange to us, and unjust. Especially when we learned that some of our close cousins—squirrels, for instance, and rabbits—were well liked. But people think we spread diseases, and I suppose possibly we do, though never intentionally, and surely we never spread as many diseases as people themselves do.—Robert C. O'Brien, *Mrs Frisby and the Rats of NIMH*, 159

Had he not become Rat Man, someone else would have.—Paul West, *Rat Man of Paris*, 8

FACING PAGE: *Rat skeleton. Photograph by Rosamond Wolff Purcell.*

freddy the rat perishes

last night he made a break at freddy
the rat keep your distance
little one said freddy i m not
feeling well myself somebody poisoned
    some
cheese for me im as full of
death as a drug store i
feel that i am going to die anyhow
come on little torpedo come on don t
    stop
to visit and search then they
went at it and both are no more please
throw a late edition on the floor i want to
keep up with china we dropped freddy
off the fire escape into the alley with
military honors
                archy

—Don Marquis, *archy and mehitabel*, 32–33

References to rats are often not-too-subtle descriptions of human beings:

"It is only because this dirty rat is a book-writing rat that you defend him!" Michael hissed . . . "If, Mr Pullman, you behave as a rat and a skunk *here* you must always have stunk—you must always have had your home in a sewer, and have been the first cousin of the mouse!"

"You like hearing yourself talk." Pullman spoke strongly and clearly. "You do not speak well! You would not be so dependent upon *rats* and *mice* if you did. You slap better than you *speak*."

Poleman laughed. "You forgot, Michael, that you were speaking to a man trained in the use of words."

"Yes, like so many people living among words, he has grown demoralized as a man. He has no values left. They have become *words* and have been rotted. You are a *rat*."—Wyndham Lewis, *Monstre Gai*, 186

In *Rat Man of Paris*, the rat man carries around with him a rat which he proudly displays to passers-by in hopes that he will be paid something to leave:

In the old, postwar days, before his rage mellowed, he worked the streets of the city with a squad of kids, flashed his live rat at the diners and Pernod sippers on the boulevards while the kids picked pockets. In several ways his art was one of distraction. The kids supplied him with the rats, maybe one a month, and of each rat in turn he became quite fond until he set it free, usually in Pigalle, with a brisk tap of his foot. The rats never came back, and of course the odds against his getting the same rat to work with him again were vast. Yet some of them seemed oddly familiar to him, and he could never be sure, so he treated them all as old allies. Never has he been bitten.—Paul West, *Rat Man of Paris*, 6

De Gier stroked the rat.

"Leave the varmint alone," Grijpstra said. "Rats are loaded with disease. Ah, that's another thing, we've got to wash him too."

"Consider it done." De Gier turned on a faucet. The rat rattled excitedly. "You like that, do you?" De Gier mixed soap suds with hot water in a bowl. "Can you get in by yourself?" Eddy clambered into his bath. His head hung over the edge while de Gier kneaded the wet little body gently. The rat's rattle became louder.

"Now what?" Grijpstra asked. "He just ate a quarter-pound of cheese. Hungry again?"

"Limited program," de Gier said. "Probably expressing positive emotion now. Rats can't talk, you know."—Janwillem Van de Wetering, *The Rattle-Rat*, 71

Hardly had the light been extinguished, when a peculiar trembling began to affect the netting under which the three children lay.

It consisted of a multitude of dull scratches which produced a metallic sound, as if claws and teeth were gnawing at the copper wire. This was accompanied by all sorts of little piercing cries.

The little five-year-old boy, on hearing this hubbub overhead, and chilled with terror, jogged his brother's elbow; but the elder brother had already shut his peepers . . . Then the little one, who could no long control his terror, questioned Gavroche, but in a very low tone, and with bated breath:—

"Sir?"

"Hey?" said Gavroche, who had just closed his eyes.

"What is that?"

"It's the rats," replied Gavroche.

And he laid his head down on the mat again.

The rats, in fact, who swarmed by thousands . . . had been held in awe by the flame of the candle, so long as it had been lighted; but as soon as the cavern, which was the same as their city, had returned to darkness, scenting what the good story-teller Perrault calls "fresh meat," they had hurled themselves in throngs on Gavroche's tent, had climbed to the top of it, and had begun to bite the meshes as though seeking to pierce this new-fangled trap.

Shakespeare's many references to rats include mentions in the following plays:

As You Like It. Act III, Scene II

Hamlet. Act III, Scene IV

King Lear. Act III, Scene IV

Macbeth. Act I, Scene III

The Merchant of Venice. Act I, Scene III

The Merry Wives of Windsor. Act II, Scene II

Romeo and Juliet. Act III, Scene I

The Tempest. Act I, Scene II

Hmmmmm, what's that group of rats doing over there near the Learned Professor's file-card cabinet? Rats lined up, going in one at a time. Familiar smell in the air as I creep closer . . .

The rebels are using the file cabinet for their official toilet! Oh, the bastards! The precious drawers have been opened and pissed into, causing the ink to run. Whole passages have been eradicated. You have no decency, fellow rats. You have no boundaries. You're going too far this time, and somehow the brave toilet-trained Doctor Rat will stop you.—William Kotzwinkle, *Doctor Rat*, 124

Paris would be dull indeed with only one amphitheater, the Roman Arènes de Lutèce, and all it took was one good man crazy in love with his cat to set the plans in emotion on a chosen construction site. Señor Le Brun simply wanted a cultivated setting in which to promenade his cat Tobermory—who'd have none of such nonsense but swiftly cleared the area of its notorious rats.*

*One of these, known to the Buffon crowd as Le Grand Crème, had been wreaking considerable havoc among the cheese shops of the area, so in gratitude, the cheese merchants scratched up some coins to toss into the arena project as well. With its fast-growing international prestige, the cheese dealers take great pride in their neighborhood cultural center, and sponsor occasional comedy nights they call La Vache Qui Rit, after the Laughing Cow merchandise they hawk so liberally.—Karen Elizabeth Gordon, Paris Out of Hand, 55–56

Still the little one could not sleep.

"Sir?" he began again.

"Hey?" said Gavroche.

"What are rats?"

"They are mice."

This explanation reassured the child a little. He had seen white mice in the course of his life, and he was not afraid of them. Nevertheless, he lifted up his voice once more.

"Sir?"

"Hey?" said Gavroche again.

"Why don't you have a cat?"

"I did have one," replied Gavroche, "I brought one here, but they ate her."

This second explanation undid the work of the first, and the little fellow began to tremble again.

The dialogue between him and Gavroche began again for the fourth time:—

"Monsieur?"

"Hey?"

"Who was it that was eaten?"

"The cat."

"And who ate the cat?"

"The rats."

"The mice?"

"Yes, the rats."

The child, in consternation, dismayed at the thought of mice which ate cats, pursued:—

"Sir, would those mice eat us?"

"Wouldn't they just!"—Victor Hugo, Les Misérables, 135–36

A detail from J. J. Grandville's illustration of la Fontaine's fable "Le rat et l'éléphant" ("The Rat and the Elephant").

I slept about two hours, and dreamed I was at home with my wife and children, which aggravated my sorrows when I awaked, and found myself alone in a vast room, between two and three hundred feet wide, and above two hundred high, lying in a bed twenty yards wide . . . While I was under these circumstances, two rats crept up the curtains and ran smelling backwards and forwards on the bed. One of them came up almost to my face, whereupon I rose in a fright, and drew out my hanger to defend myself. These horrible animals had the boldness to attack me on both sides, and one of them held his fore-feet at my collar; but I had the good fortune to rip up his belly before he could do me mischief. He fell down at my feet, and the other, seeing the fate of his comrade, made his escape, but not without one good wound on the back, which I gave him as he fled, and made the blood run trickling from him . . . I measured the tail of the dead rat, and found it to be two yards long, wanting an inch; but it went against my stomach to drag the carcass off the bed, where it lay still bleeding . . .

Soon after, my mistress came into the room, who, seeing me all bloody, ran and took me up in her hand. I pointed to the dead rat, smiling, and making other signs, to shew I was not hurt, whereat she was extremely rejoiced, calling the maid to take up the dead rat with a pair of tongs and throw it out the window.—Jonathan Swift, *Gulliver's Travels*, 78–79

One of Nabokov's novels has a scene that highlights the gothic virtues of the brothel known as the Villa Venus:

The grand piano in the otherwise bare hall seemed to be playing all by itself but actually was being rippled by rats in quest of the succulent refuse placed there by the maid who fancied a bit of music when her cancered womb roused her before dawn with its first familiar stab. The ruinous Villa no longer bore any resemblance to Eric's "organized dream," but the soft little creature in Van's desperate grasp was Ada.—Vladimir Nabokov, *Ada*, 358

On the fifth floor the door on the right opened a few inches and Perico saw a gigantic rat in a white nightgown peeking out with one eye and all of her nose. Before she could close the door again, he stuck his shoe in and recited for her that thing that among serpents, the basilisk had an organ so poisonous for all the others and so overwhelming that he frightened them just by hissing and they scattered and fled at his coming, he could kill them with his glance.—Julio Cortázar, *Hopscotch*, 354

6. GOTHIC RATS AND OTHER TERRORS

Gothic horror appeals to readers young and old alike, and rats magnify the terror that we feel while reading of dungeons, torture chambers, vampires and the unknown. We automatically list the names of authors such as Edgar Allan Poe and Bram Stoker when we think of Gothic horror. Indeed, both Poe and Stoker have written quintessential horror, but there is a wider world of horror awaiting us, and much of it involves rats.

> The scene upon which we intruded was ferociously original, if for no other reason than that the light, pushing up from the mud floor, touched out the eyebrows and lips and cheek-bones of the participants while it left great patches of shadow on their faces—so that they looked as if they had been half-eaten by the rats which one could hear scrambling among the rafters of this wretched tenement. It was a house of child prostitutes.
>
> —Lawrence Durrell, *Justine*, 42

Forcing herself closer, [Blanche] leaned forward and reached out her hand. But then she pulled it back sharply, thinking she had seen a movement, a faint, flickering alteration in the white folds of the cloth. She told herself, it was only a trick of the light, the shadow of her moving hand. But her imagination had already begun to conjure up new horrors, things much worse than the dead bird at lunchtime. It insisted that the tray contained something alive—a live rat, writhing and kicking in a trap! Returning her hand to the wheel of her chair, she began to back away again toward the shadows.—Henry Farrell, *Whatever Happened to Baby Jane?*, 56

Those rats that come out of our eyes as if we dwelled in tombs.—Georges Bataille, *The Impossible: A Story of Rats*, 38

This diagram from the U.S. Land Survey of the late nineteenth century shows the most feared feature of the rat—its incisors.

FACING PAGE: *Photograph by Stephen Dalton/ NHPA.*

[Temple] flung her hands out and caught herself upright, a hand on either angle of the corner, her face not twelve inches from the cross beam on which the rat crouched. For an instant they stared eye to eye, then its eyes glowed suddenly like two tiny electric bulbs and it leaped at her head just as she sprang backward, treading again on something that rolled under her foot.—William Faulkner, *Sanctuary*, 111

"I need the money," Wisconsky said. "But Christ Jesus, buddy, this ain't no work for a *man*. Those rats." He looked around fearfully. "It almost seems like they think. You ever wonder how it'd be, if we was little and they were big—"—Stephen King, "Graveyard Shift," *Night Shift*, 44

Jerzy Kosinksi's novel *The Painted Bird* has been called autobiographical. If so, the following excerpt relates a scene that surpasses most fiction for its absolute horror. The main character, an orphan, has been roped to a cart by his guardian and dragged along to a subterranean bunker. When the guardian, a carpenter, opens the hatch, they both look in and are assaulted by the stench and sight of hundreds of rats. It then becomes clear to the horrified boy that he is about to be thrown in, so he takes steps to make sure that it is the carpenter and not he who falls to a grisly death:

The massive body of the carpenter was only partly visible. His face and half of his arms were lost under the surface of the sea of rats, and wave after wave of rats was scrambling over his belly and legs. The man completely disappeared, and the sea of rats churned even more violently. The moving rumps of the rats became stained with brownish red blood. The animals now fought for access to the body—panting, twitching their tails, their teeth gleaming under their half-open snouts, their eyes reflecting the daylight as if they were the beads of a rosary.

. . . suddenly the momentum of the surging animals thrust to the surface the entire bluish-white skeleton of the carpenter, partly defleshed and partly covered with shreds of reddish skin and gray clothing. In between the ribs, under the armpits, and in the place where the belly was, gaunt rodents fiercely struggled for the remaining scraps of dangling muscle and intestine. Mad with greed, they tore from one another scraps of clothing, skin, and formless chunks of the trunk. They dived into the center of the man's body only to jump out through another chewed hole. The corpse sank under renewed thrusts. When it next came to the surface of the bloody writhing sludge, it was a completely bare skeleton.—Jerzy Kosinski, *The Painted Bird*, 64–65

The terrifying threat of being eaten alive by rats is a theme that occurs time and again. H. P. Lovecraft and George Orwell both wrote about it:

Kephren was their leader; sneering King Khephren *or the guide Abdul Reis*, crowned with a golden pshent and intoning endless formulae with the hollow voice of the dead. By his side knelt beautiful Queen Nitokris, whom I saw in profile for a moment, noting that the right half of her face was eaten away by rats or other ghouls.—H.P. Lovecraft, "Under the Pyramid," 241

Something bumped into me—something soft and plump. It must have been the rats; the viscous, gelatinous, ravenous army that feast on the dead and the living . . .

. . . they found me in the blackness after three hours; found me crouching in the blackness over the plump, half-eaten body of Capt. Norrys, with my own cat leaping and tearing at my throat. Now they have blown up Exham Priory . . . and shut me into this barred room at Hanwell with fearful whispers about my heredity and experiences . . . When I speak of poor Norrys they accuse me of a hideous thing, but they must know that I did not do it. They must know it was the rats; the slithering, scurrying rats whose scampering will never let me sleep; the dæmon rats that race behind the padding in this room and beckon me down to greater horrors than I have ever known; the rats they can never hear; the rats, the rats in the walls.—H.P. Lovecraft, "Rats in the Wall," 44–45

Suddenly the foul musty odor of the brutes struck his nostrils. There was a violent convulsion of nausea inside him, and he almost lost consciousness. Everything had gone black. For an instant he was insane, a screaming animal . . .

"It was a common punishment in Imperial China," said O'Brien as didactically as ever.

The mask was closing on his face. The wire brushed his cheek. And then—no, it was not relief, only hope, a tiny fragment of hope. Too late, perhaps too late. But he had suddenly understood that in the whole world there was just *one* person to whom he could transfer his punishment . . .

Well, have they not managed to graft the tail from one rat's body on to another living rat's back? Try then, similarly, to transport the several modifications of my cadaverous reason into your imagination.—Comte de Lautréamont, *Maldoror*, 180

Streets that run back from the docks with their tattered rotten supercargo of houses, breathing into each other's mouths, keeling over. Shuttered balconies swarming with rats.—Lawrence Durrell, *Justine*, 26

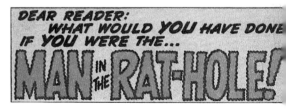

From Tower of Shadows: *TM and Copyright © 1960, Marvel Characters, Inc. All Rights Reserved.*

Of all horrors in the world—a rat!
—George Orwell, *Nineteen Eighty-four*, 145

Gustave Doré's illustration from La légende de Croque-Mitaine (The Legend of the Bogey Man), *text by Ernest L'Epine, first published 1863.*

"The rat always went up the rope of the alarm bell?"

"Always."

"I suppose you know," said the Doctor after a pause, "what the rope is?"

"No!"

"It is," said the Doctor slowly, "the very rope which the hangman used for all the victims of the Judge's judicial rancour!"—Bram Stoker, "The Judge's House," 35

And he was shouting frantically, over and over:

"Do it to Julia! Do it to Julia! Not me! Julia! I don't care what you do to her. Tear her face off, strip her to the bones. Not me! Julia! Not me!"—George Orwell, *Nineteen Eighty-four*, 288–89

In Edgar Allan Poe's story "The Pit and the Pendulum," rats are the heroes as they chew through the rope holding the unnamed narrator (given the name Francis Barnard in the movie) prisoner in a Spanish Inquisitor's dungeon. However, in the 1961 movie version, directed by Roger Corman and starring Vincent Price, rats are replaced by humans and the Inquisition prison becomes a madman's torture chamber. We see only a few rats crawling about as Vincent Price walks down into the dungeon. But here is Poe's version:

For many hours the immediate vicinity of the low framework upon which I lay, had been literally swarming with rats. They were wild, bold, ravenous; their red eyes glaring upon me as if they waited but for motionlessness on my part to make me their prey. "To what food," I thought, "have they been accustomed in the well?"

They had devoured, in spite of all my efforts to prevent them, all but a small remnant of the contents of the dish. I had fallen into an habitual see-saw, or wave of the hand about the platter: and, at length, the unconscious uniformity of the movement deprived it of effect. In their voracity the vermin frequently fastened their sharp fangs in my fingers. With the particles of the oily and spicy viand which now remained, I thoroughly rubbed the bandage wherever I could reach it; then, raising my hand from the floor, I lay breathlessly still.

At first the ravenous animals were startled and terrified at the change—at the cessation of movement. They shrank alarmedly back; many sought the well. But this was only for a moment. I had not counted in vain upon their voracity. Observing that I remained without motion, one or two of the boldest leaped upon the framework, and smelt at the surcingle. This seemed the signal for a general rush. Forth from the well they hurried in fresh troops. They clung to the wood—they overran it, and leaped in hundreds upon my person. The measured movement of the pendulum disturbed them not at all. Avoiding its strokes they busied them-selves with the anointed bandage. They pressed—they swarmed upon me in ever accumulating heaps. They writhed upon my throat; their cold lips sought my own; I was half stifled by their thronging pressure; disgust, for which the world has no name, swelled my bosom, and chilled, with a heavy clamminess, my heart. Yet one minute, and I felt that the struggle would be over.—Edgar Allan Poe, "The Pit and the Pendulum," 319–20

He lay on the bed like an embalmed gargoyle. He was naked and his whole body was black with dried blood. There was a dark halo on the sheet around his neck and head which was obviously caused by the blood that had run from the wound in his throat. His neck had been slit from ear to ear, the wound grinned at us like a second mouth. There was a knife clutched in his left hand, glinting in the golden light, blood on silver. His whole body was encrusted with flies and maggots like a second skin. Three rats were nibbling at various parts of his body, and, as we looked, a fourth jumped on to the bed and stared at us like a gloating succubus . . . The Devil lay there like a sacrifice.—Philip Ridley, *In the Eyes of Mister Fury*, 26

There on the great high-backed carved oak chair by the right side of the fire-place sat an enormous rat, steadily glaring at him with baleful eyes. He made a motion to it as though to hunt it away, but it did not stir. Then he made the motion of throwing something. Still it did not stir, but showed

This lurid cover for *The Coming of the Rats* by George H. Smith (VanNuys: Pike Books, 1961) fully illustrates the horror of a rat attack.

You know the keen face of a rat, those two sharp teeth, those pitiless eyes. Seen magnified to near six times its linear dimensions, and still more magnified by darkness and amaze-ment and the leaping fancies of a fitful blaze, it must have been an ill sight.— H.G. Wells, *The Food of the Gods*, 63

61

And where were Skinner's boots, for example? Perverted and strange as a rat's appetite must be, is it conceivable that the same creatures that could leave a lamb only half eaten, would finish up Skinner—hair, bones, teeth, and boots?—H.G. Wells, *The Food of the Gods,* 58

"You will observe," said the commissary to the officer and to me as he took out his note book, "that the woman must have fallen on her dagger. The rats are many here—see their eyes glistening among that heap of bones—and you will also notice"—I shuddered as he placed his hand on the skeleton—"that but little time was lost by them, for the bones are scarcely cold!"—Bram Stoker, "The Burial of the Rats," 153

its great white teeth angrily, and its cruel eyes shone in the lamplight with an added vindictiveness.

Malcomson felt amazed, and seizing the poker from the hearth ran at it to kill it. Before, however, he could strike it, the rat, with a squeak that sounded like the concentration of hate, jumped upon the floor, and, running up the rope of the alarm bell, disappeared in the darkness beyond the range of the green-shaded lamp. Instantly, strange to say, the noisy scampering of the rats in the wainscot began again.—Bram Stoker, "The Judge's House," 27

A few minutes later I saw Morris step suddenly back from a corner, which he was examining. We all followed his movements with our eyes, for undoubtedly some nervousness was growing on us, and we saw a whole mass of phosphorescence, which twinkled like stars. We all instinctively drew back. The whole place was becoming alive with rats.

For a moment or two we stood appalled, all save Lord Godalming, who was seemingly prepared for such an emergency. Rushing over to the great iron-bound oaken door, which Dr Seward had described from the outside, and which I had seen myself, he turned the key in the lock, drew the huge bolts, and swung the door open. Then, taking his little silver whistle from his pocket, he blew a low, shrill call. It was answered from behind Dr Seward's house by the yelping of dogs, and after about a minute three terriers came dashing round the corner of the house . . . But even in the minute that had elapsed the number of rats had vastly increased. They seemed to swarm over the place all at once, till the lamplight, shining on their moving dark bodies and glittering, baleful eyes, made the place look like a bank of earth set with fireflies. The dogs dashed on, but at the threshold suddenly stopped and snarled, and then, simultaneously lifting their noses, began to howl in most lugubrious fashion. The rats were multiplying in thousands, and we moved out.

Lord Godalming lifted one of the dogs and carrying him in, placed him on the floor. The instant his feet touched the ground he seemed to recover his courage, and rushed at his natural enemies. They fled before him so fast that before he had shaken the life out of a score, the other dogs, who had by now been lifted in the same manner, had but small prey ere the whole mass had vanished.

With their going it seemed as if some evil presence had departed, for the dogs frisked about and barked merrily as they made sudden darts at their prostrate foes, and turned them over and over and tossed them in the air with vicious shakes.—Bram Stoker, *Dracula*, 324–25

There was no need for [Barquentine] to dress. He slept in his clothes on a lice-infested mattress. There was no bed; just the crawling mattress on the carpetless floor-boards where cockroaches and beetles burrowed and insects of all kinds lived, bred and died, and where the midnight rat sat upright in the silver dust and bared its long teeth to the pale beams, when in its fullness the moon filled up the midnight window like an abstract of itself in a picture frame.—Mervyn Peake, *Gormenghast*, 161

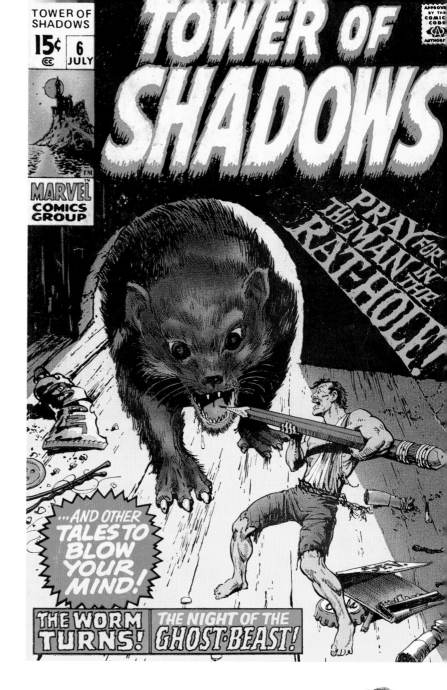

7. THE CINEMATIC RAT

The few movies made specifically about rats have either been B-horrors such as *Willard* and its sequel *Ben* or cute animated children's movies. Digging deeply through the shelves of the video stores and the listings of such filmographies as *Halliwell's Film Guide* and *Terror on Tape* has revealed a diverse selection of movies, both good and bad, that depict rats in some form or other.

Some of the following movies are difficult to obtain. An asterisk beside the title indicates that it is readily available on video.

The Abominable Dr Phibes *, 1971, starring Vincent Price as Dr Phibes and Joseph Cotten as Dr Vesalius. Dr Phibes, disfigured and rendered mute in a car accident, is a musical genius and scholar. He plans to murder the surgeons, including Dr Vesalius, responsible for the death of his wife—each is to die from one of the ten curses of the Pharaohs, and rats are one of those curses. Leslie Halliwell quotes the *Motion Picture Guide*: "The sets are awful, the plot ludicrous and the dialogue inane—what more could a horror freak desire?"

A sequel, *Doctor Phibes Rises Again* *, was made in 1972 and also stars Vincent Price.

Ben *, 1972, made as a sequel to *Willard*, is about a sickly young boy, Danny (played by Lee Harcourt Montgomery), who adopts Ben, savvy leader of a large rat pack. It also stars Arthur O'Connell and Joseph Campanella. The movie begins with the rat Ben biting his human friend Willard Sikes. Willard prepares a batch of poison in revenge, but Ben, who can read the label on the box, alerts his buddies, and Willard dies, bitten to death by his former allies. Danny's subsequent friendship with Ben is shattered by the city's efforts to eradicate the rats.

"Rats! Rats! Rats! Thousands. Millions of them."—Renfield to Dr Seward in *Dracula*

Ten plagues from Exodus 9:3: River runs with blood, frogs, lice, flies, murrain*, boils, hail, locusts, darkness, first born.

Ten plagues from *Dr Phibes*: Boils, bats, frogs, blood, rats, hail, beasts, locusts, death of first born, darkness.

*Murrain: any of the plagues or illnesses that strike livestock.

FACING PAGE: *Indiana Jones (Harrison Ford) and Dr Elsa Schneider (Alison Doody) pick their way through a sea of rats in* Indiana Jones and the Last Crusade™ & © *Lucasfilm Ltd. (LFL), 1989. All Rights Reserved. Courtesy of Lucasfilm Ltd. Still from BFI Stills, Posters and Designs.*

All About Eve, 1950

"Playing that childish game of cat and mouse."

"Mouse. Not mouse. If anything—rat."

—Lloyd Richards (Hugh Marlowe) and Margo Channing (Bette Davis)

Annie Get Your Gun, 1950

Howard Keel sings to Betty Hutton that he can live on bread and cheese. She responds, "Only on that? So can a rat!"—"Anything You Can Do I Can Do Better" by Irving Berlin

Famous last words from *Ben*, 1972

"You afraid of rats?"

"Nah, they're easy to handle. Give them a chance and they'll always run away from you."

"I know that, and you know that, but do *they* know that?"

—Two police officers about to enter Willard Sike's house to search for rats

A Star Is Born, 1937

"There go a couple of rats I raised from mice."—Mack Haines, publicity agent, about Vicki Lester (Janet Gaynor) and co-star and new husband Norman Maine (Frederic March)

Blood and Donuts, 1995, a Canadian film starring Gordon Currie, Justin Louise, Helene Clarkson and Fiona Reid, with a cameo appearance by David Cronenberg. A vampire who went into hibernation at the time of the first walk on the moon returns to life in modern-day Toronto. Rats provide the atmosphere.

Bram Stoker's Burial of the Rats, 1995, a Roger Corman Presents production: It has to do with a woman who has certain powers over rats . . . it is quite obviously an excuse for a large number of buxom women to dance about in fur thong bikinis while Barbeau, tooting on a magic flute that gives her power over Mickey Mouse's relatives growls such lines as, "I am the Queen of Vermin, the Pied Piper's twisted sister!" It's all bosoms and buns, straight sex and lesbian jealousy with just enough gore thrown in to justify calling it a horror movie.—Ken Schactman and Danny Savello, "Roger Redux," *Scarlet Street*, Fall 1995, 31

Charly *, 1968, based on the Daniel Keyes novel *Flowers for Algernon*.

Deadly Eyes *, 1982, directed by Robert Clouse and starring Sam Groom, Sara Botsford and Scatman Crothers, based on the novel *The Rats* by James Herbert. A colony of rats has grown into monsters after feeding on grain laced with potent steroids. They search for food via the tunnels of the Toronto subway system. According to James O'Neill, the rats are "played by dachshunds in rat suits . . . listen closely and you can even hear some of them barking!"—*Terror on Tape*, 95

Diamonds Are Forever *, 1971, based on the novel by Ian Fleming and starring Sean Connery and Jill St John. An unconscious James Bond (Sean Connery) is dumped into a pipe lying in a construction site. Later on in the day a construction crew arrives and finishes off the sewer line, enclosing Bond in an underground tunnel. He wakes up to find his only company is a rat. After looking around for a second or two, he sniffs the air, saying, "One of us smells like a tart's handkerchief." He then sniffs again and says, "I'm afraid that's me. Sorry about that, old boy."

Dracula *, 1931. Rats show up early in this well-crafted and faithful version of the Dracula story. They make their way in and out of coffins in Count Dracula's dungeon, crawling over resting vampires.

In the following scene, the dialogue is close to that of the book:

Renfield to Dr Seward and Dr van Helsing (Edward Van Sloan):

"A red mist spread over the lawn, coming on like a flame of fire and then he parted it. And I could see that there were thousands of rats with their eyes blazing red like his, only smaller. And then he held up his hand, and they all stopped. And I thought he seemed to be saying, 'Rats! Rats! Rats! Thousands. Millions of them. All red-blood, all these will I give you if you will obey me.'"

"What did he want you to do?"

"That which has already been done."

Ralph Meeker is overcome by a giant rat in Food of the Gods, *1976.*

Food of the Gods, 1976, based on the original story by H.G. Wells, starring Marjoe Gortner, Pamela Franklin, Ida Lupino and Ralph Meeker. Something oozing out of the ground on Ida Lupino's Canadian farm turns common beasts—rats, worms, chickens, wasps—into giant monsters. The film bears little resemblance to the original. "I wish I hadn't seen the movie, so I could avoid it like the plague."—John Simon, in *Halliwell's Film Guide*

Food of the Gods II, 1989, starring Paul Coufos, Lisa Schrage and Jackie Burroughs. This was neither a sequel to the first nor another version of H.G. Wells's original story. Giant rats invade a university campus following hormone experiments gone awry. The highlight is a rat attack on a team of synchronized swimmers.

The Deer Hunter, 1978, directed by Michael Cimino and starring Robert De Niro. A soldier is captured by the Viet Cong and put into a watery pit. While he is trapped, rats crawl around and over him.

CAMEO

The Desert Rats, 1953. Not really a rat movie. An English captain who commands an Australian detachment in the siege of Tobruk survives an encounter with Rommel. The only rats are the Desert Rats military unit.

3-D CAMEO

Friday the 13th, Part 3, 1982. Directed by Steve Miner, written by Martin Kitrosser and Carol Watson. Starring Dana Kimmel, Paul Kratka and Richard Brooker as Jason. The cameo appearance of this rat was intensified by the 3-D effects featured in the film.

Indiana Jones and the Last Crusade, 1989
"Wouldn't it have been wonderful if your father were here to see this?"
"Never would have made it past the rats. He hates rats. Scared to death of them."
—Indiana Jones to Dr Elsa Schneider about his father, Holy Grail scholar Henry Jones (Sean Connery)

From Russia with Love*, 1963, starring Sean Connery as James Bond and Pedro Armendariz as Kerim. This classic James Bond thriller set in Istanbul remains quite true to the Ian Fleming novel of the same title.

Graveyard Shift*, 1990, based on the short story of the same name by Stephen King. This movie, directed by Ralph Singleton, is about a group of textile-mill employees who are sent down into the pits during the graveyard shift to clean up a rat infestation. They discover underground tunnels leading to the cemetery and suffer a fate worse than death.

Indiana Jones and the Last Crusade*, 1989, the last in the trio of Indiana Jones movies, directed by Steven Spielberg and written by George Lucas. Indiana Jones (Harrison Ford) and Dr Elsa Schneider (Alison Doody) make their way through a rat-infested catacomb under the library in Venice. Thousands of rats mill about their feet and drop down onto their shoulders. When they first encounter the rodents, Indiana Jones's first word is "Rats!"

King Rat*, 1961, based on the novel by James Clavell, starring George Segal as King and James Fox as Peter Marlowe. An excellent adaptation of the book.

Last Tango in Paris*, 1972, a Bernardo Bertolucci movie starring Marlon Brando and Maria Schneider. Finding a rat in this movie was, frankly, a surprise. Jeanne (Maria Schneider) enters the bedroom she shares occasionally with Paul (Marlon Brando). She discovers a dead rat on the bed, which Paul picks up and uses to tease her:

> PAUL: Rat. Only a rat. More rats in Paris than people. Num num num . . .
>
> JEANNE: I want to go! I want . . .
>
> PAUL: Don't you want a bite first? You don't want to run and eat?
>
> JEANNE: This is the end!
>
> PAUL: No, this is the end (points at rat's bottom). But I like to start with the head; that's the best part. Are you sure you won't have any? Okay (holds rat above his open mouth). What's the matter, you don't dig rat?

Little Criminals, 1996, CBC, directed by Stephen Sergik and written by Dennis Foon. Starring Brendan Fletcher, Myles Ferguson and Amy Kuzyk. Animal training by Debbie Coe and special rat effects by John Sleep. In this chronicle of the lives of a group of youths in Vancouver, the children film themselves stealing a gun in a break-in and then going down to the waterfront to shoot rats.

Murder in the First*, 1995, directed by Marc Rocco and written by Dan Gorder. Kevin Bacon stars as Henri Young, a young man convicted and sent to the darkest reaches of Alcatraz for the crime of stealing $5 to feed his starving sister. After making a failed attempt at escape, he's stripped and thrown into a hole without light where he is confined for three years. His only companion for the entire time is a rat that he allows to sit on his leg.

1984*, 1984, based on the novel *Nineteen Eighty-four* by George Orwell, starring John Hurt as Winston Smith and Richard Burton as O'Brien. Rats are significant throughout the movie as powerful motifs of Winston's fear of death. They first appear in dreamlike flashbacks of childhood, crawling about on the corpse of Winston's mother, and then swarming through the empty flat that was

Mark of the Vampire, 1935. Directed by Tod Browning and starring Lionel Barrymore, Jean Hersholt and Bela Lugosi. This good-looking but ridiculous movie received high marks amongst horror film aficionados—largely due to the cinematography of James Wong Howe. Vaudeville performers pose as vampires in an effort to expose the real murderer of a wealthy landowner. Rats are bit-players in this movie.

CAMEO

ALL IN A NAME
Midnight Cowboy, 1969. The rat in this film was the human Ratso Rizzo, played by Dustin Hoffman.

Mr Lucky, 1943
"I thought we had rat guards on this ship. How did you get on?"
—The Crunk (Cary Grant's henchman) to Zep (untrustworthy, former business partner played by Paul Stewart) on board Cary Grant's ship.

Nightmares, 1983. Four horror episodes rolled into one movie directed by Joseph Sargent. The rat sequence stars Veronica Cartwright and Richard Masur as a couple who find their home taken over by a huge rat.

Nosferatu the Vampyre, 1979

"Wait, the Master is coming."

"Who is coming? Tell us more."

"The Master of the Rats. The army of rats is hungry and 400,000 strong."

—The mad Renfield to Lucy about the powers of Nosferatu

On the Waterfront, 1955

"Stooling is when you rat on your friends."—Union lackey to Terry Malloy (Marlon Brando)

CAMEO

Phantom of the Opera, 1925. In this first version of the Phantom story, Lon Chaney plays a disfigured man in a mask. He abducts the prima donna of the Paris Opera House and takes her to his lair in the sewers below. There are no rats, but the rat-catcher appears, enigmatically exhorting those searching for her not to look at him: "I am the messenger from the shadows: turn back ere ye perish."

Poster from the movie Nosferatu, *1921, by Albin Grau. Courtesy of David J. Skal,* Hollywood Gothic.

his home. But the *pièce de résistance* is the torture scene in which O'Brien, who has discovered Winston's hatred and fear of rats, has devised a helmetlike cage to be fitted over the face. It contains two rats separated from the face by a removable grille. The dialogue is true to the book:

"I have pressed the first lever," said O'Brien. "You understand the construction of this cage. The mask will fit over your head, leaving no exit. When I press this other lever, the door of the cage will slide up. These starving brutes will shoot out of it like bullets. Have you ever seen a rat leap through the air? They will leap onto your face and bore straight into it. Sometimes they attack the eyes first. Sometimes they burrow through the cheeks and devour the tongue."

Nosferatu*, 1921, a silent film starring Max Schreck as Count Orlok—the vampire Nosferatu. Thomas Hutter (Gustav von Wangenheim) goes to Orlok's castle in the Carpathian Mountains to offer him a piece of property in the town of Wisborg. The castle is marvellously atmospheric, with a skeleton chime clock and doors that open unaided. As in the 1931 Dracula movie, rats appear milling about the vampires' coffins, on board the ship and swarming the docks as the ship lands.

Nosferatu the Vampyre*, 1979, written and directed by Werner Herzog and starring Klaus Kinski as Nosferatu, Isabelle Adjani as Lucy and Bruno Ganz as Jonathan Harker. Rats are a big feature in this version of Dracula—they're everywhere. But particularly bizarre is a scene that takes place in the town square—the plague has struck the town, brought by Nosferatu's rats, and a family dines formally in the middle of the square with rats milling about at the foot of the table. When dinner is abandoned, the rats take over.

Of Unknown Origin, 1983, based on the novel *The Visitor* by Chauncey G. Parker III, directed by George Cosmatos and starring Peter Weller, Shannon Tweed and Jennifer Dale. A New York brownstone is invaded by a smart, powerful and giant rat. Close-ups of the eyes and claws add to the sense of horror in this movie.

The Pied Piper, 1971, starring Donovan, Donald Pleasance and John Hurt. This film did not receive much critical acclaim despite its cast. It is about—what else—the Pied Piper legend.

The Princess Bride, 1987. This Rob Reiner film is a fairy tale in which the two main characters encounter rodents the size of German shepherd dogs in a forest of deadly traps.

The Rats, 1983. This Italian-made movie starring Richard Raymond, Alex McBride and Richard Cross, directed by Vincent Dawn, features people living in a postnuclear-war world with man-eating rats.

Some Kind of Hero*, 1981, starring Richard Pryor as Eddie Keller, a Vietnam POW who befriends a rat he calls Spike.

Taras Bulba*, 1962, directed by J. Lee-Thompson, starring Yul Brynner and Tony Curtis. Starving prisoners in a sixteenth-century Ukrainian castle wait in silence ready to pounce on rats—perhaps their only source of food. An added

Phantom of the Opera, 1943, starring Claude Rains and Nelson Eddy. Rats appear in the sewers under the Paris Opera. They are there for atmosphere but are not used to great effect. *Phantom of the Opera* was also remade in 1962 and 1989.

CAMEO

The Princess Comes Across, 1936 "To catch a rat you've got to have cheese!"

—King Mantell (Fred MacMurray) to the so-called Princess Olga (Carole Lombard) as they try to catch a shipboard murderer

Prospero's Books, 1991, written and directed by Peter Greenaway, and starring John Gielgud. Rats appear as part of the amazing background of corruption, lechery and magic.

CAMEO

Saturday Night and Sunday Morning, 1960, based on the novel by Alan Sillitoe. Albert Finney, as Arthur, takes a dead rat presented to him by the factory cat, stuffs it down his shirt and dumps it onto a co-worker's bench. She sets up a huge fuss when she discovers it. Arthur is immediately suspected. In the novel, the rat is a mouse, not nearly as visually effective.

CAMEO

CAMEO

The Shawshank Redemption, 1995, directed by Frank Durabont and based on the novella "Rita Hayworth and the Shawshank Redemption" by Stephen King. A rat runs by the solitary cell of inmate Andy Dusfresne (Tim Robbins).

CAMEO

Tower of London, 1962, directed by Roger Corman and starring Vincent Price as Richard III. Also stars Michael Pate, Joan Freeman and Bruce Gordon. Richard III stops at nothing on his rise to the throne. Among other tortures, he throws a man to the rats.

CAMEO

Whatever Happened to Baby Jane, 1962, based on the novel by Henry Farrell about two quarrelling sisters. Bette Davis serves up a rat for lunch to the terrified Blanche (Joan Crawford).

CAMEO

Wild Beasts, 1983, directed by Franco Prosperi and starring Lorraine de Selle, John Aldrich and Ugo Bologna. Set in Berlin, this Italian movie follows the animals of the Berlin Zoo when they go berserk after drinking contaminated water. The rats consume a necking couple.

bonus in this overacted Cossack epic is a classic plague scene replete with dead bodies and cries of "Bring out your dead!"

Truly, Madly, Deeply*, 1990, starring Juliet Stevenson as Nina, Alan Rickman as her dead lover, Christopher Rózycki as Titus, David Ryall as George the rat exterminator and Squeak as the rat. Nina is grieving for her dead lover and trying to cope with a flat that is falling down around her. When rats appear in the house, she calls the exterminator, who lays poison bait around the place. Titus, who is fixing her cupboards, comments: "In my country when you want to be rid of rats, you do not use poison. We dance. To drive the rats away we dance."

Willard, 1971, based on the novel *Ratman's Notebooks* by Stephen Gilbert, starring Bruce Davison as Willard, Ernest Borgnine as Martin, and Sondra Locke. (Sondra Locke also stars in a 1986 movie called *Ratboy*.) The rat trainer is Moe de Sesso. Willard Sikes trains rats to avenge his family's misfortunes. Martin, the focus of his hatred, eventually dies at the teeth of the army of rats. "Only horrifying to people who can't stand rats."—*Halliwell's Film Guide*, 1996

Hard to find or hard to watch

The Rat, 1925, France, silent. Starring Ivor Novello.

The Rat, 1937, France. A Parisian thief takes the blame for a murder, but is saved by the socialite who loves him. Starring Anton Walbrook and Ruth Chatterton.

Les Rat des Villes et le Rat des Champs, 1927, France, animation.

Rat Life and Diet in North America, 1968, Canada. A short film by artist Joyce Wieland.

Ratboy, 1986, U.S.A. A half-rodent alien gets the anticipated rough treatment when he visits earth.

Die Ratten, 1955, Germany. Starring Maria Schell and Curt Jurgens.

Documentary

Ratopolis*, 1994, written and directed by Gilles Thérien. A documentary about *Rattus norvegicus*, showing how they live in controlled environments and in the wild. Also an overview of historic attitudes towards rats.

Movies About Plague

The Devils*, 1970, written and directed by Ken Russell from the book *The Devils of Loudun* by Aldous Huxley, starring Vanessa Redgrave and Oliver Reed. There are actually no rats in this movie, in spite of ideal conditions.

Four Frightened People, 1934, directed by Cecil B. de Mille. An outbreak of bubonic plague terrorizes Claudette Colbert and Herbert Marshall. Four of the survivors escape in a life boat and head for safety into the jungle.

Isle of the Dead, 1945, directed by Mark Robson and starring Boris Karloff, Ellen Drew and Jason Robards. A group of people attempt to isolate themselves from the plague but end up fearing that one of them is a vampire.

The Masque of the Red Death*, 1964. A Roger Corman film based on the story by Edgar Allan Poe. Starring Vincent Price, Hazel Court and Patrick Magee.

The Navigator: A Medieval Odyssey, 1988. Medieval townspeople travel through time in order to escape the plague.

The Omega Man*, 1971, starring Charlton Heston and Rosalind Cash. This disaster movie is about the decimation of the world's population due to plague and the attempts of one man to fight against the carriers of the disease.

Terror Creatures from the Grave, 1965, directed by Ralph Zucker, starring Barbara Steele and Walter Brandi. Victims of the black plague are called upon to rise up from the dead to avenge the murder of a paralysed scientist.

SILLY PLAGUE

Monty Python and the Holy Grail*, 1975, starring Graham Chapman, John Cleese, Terry Gilliam, Eric Idle and Michael Palin. A scene in the movie shows the collectors of the dead heaping the bodies of those struck down by the plague into disrespectful piles.

FILM NOIR PLAGUE

Panic in the Streets*, 1950, directed by Elia Kazan, starring Jack Palance and Richard Widmark. A suspected carrier of bubonic plague is tracked down by public health officers in New Orleans.

73

8. THE FOUR DEADLY SINS

Okay, so no one creature is perfect. Humans have seven deadly sins, but rats have only four. Rats are missing out on envy, sloth and pride, but they make the most of gluttony, lechery, covetousness and wrath.

Gluttony

The destruction a brown rat can inflict on livestock, feed and vegetables goes beyond basic survival. Rather than eating one apple or one potato, a rat will take one bite out of many; and instead of being satisfied with a sufficient amount of nesting material, it will shred great amounts of clothing and printed matter. Joseph Mitchell describes the vandalism carried out by brown rats "going berserk" in warehouses, fouling and destroying entire stocks:

> One night, in the poultry part of old Gansevoort Market, alongside the Hudson, a burrow of them bit the throats of over three hundred broilers and ate less than a dozen. Before this part of the market was abandoned, in 1942, the rats practically had charge of it. Some of them nested in the drawers of desks. When the drawers were pulled open, they leaped out, snarling.—Joseph Mitchell, "The Rats on the Waterfront," 62

Well before dawn, the rue Vauvilliers smells of rumpsteak. The rat, who I have called Gaspardino, for simplicity's sake, was born with this odor in his muzzle. For the most part he thinks of nothing but eating but the meat remains inaccessible, too close to men. In order to believe himself stronger, Gaspardino lives in a group, with other thieves of his sort, and his nose sweeps the routes marked with warning signals by generations of rats.

—Patrick Rambaud, *Comme des Rats,* 9

A woman with a composite body, partly human, partly fish and hollow tree, allies the minor theme of the Siren to the major one of the hollow tree, the latter being, in alchemistic literature, a constant figure of the crucible and the Philisopher's Stone . . . This figure rides upon a rat, which Ruysbroek assimilates to all the heresies.—Jacques Combe, *Jerome Bosch,* describing the painting *The Temptation of Saint Anthony,* 87

FACING PAGE: *Detail from the central panel of* The Temptation of Saint Anthony *by Hieronymus Bosch (1505–06). By permission of the Museu Nacional de Arte Antiga, Lisbon. Photograph by José Pessoa, Arquivo Nacional de Fotografia/ Instituto Português de Museus.*

As he set foot on O'Connell bridge a puffball of smoke plumed up from the parapet. Brewery barge with export stout. England. Sea air sours it, I heard. Be interesting some day to get a pass through Hancock to see the brewery. Regular world in itself. Vats of porter, wonderful. Rats get in too. Drink themselves bloated as big as a collie floating. Dead drunk on the porter. Drink till they puke again like christians. Imagine drinking that! Rats: vats. Well of course if we knew all the things.—James Joyce, *Ulysses*, 152

J.J. Grandville illustration of the la Fontaine fable "The Hermit Rat," about a rat who was content to live in his cheese rather than help his fellow rats.

"Can you understand what the rats are saying?"

"No."

"Can you talk to them?"

"No. But I can kill them."

"Why?"

"Because they are never satisfied. They are like bad politicians and imperialists and rich people."

"How?"

"They eat up property. They eat up everything in sight. And one day when they are very hungry they will eat us up."—Ben Okri, *The Famished Road*, 233

Some of the more obvious qualities in which rats resemble men—ferocity, omnivorousness, and adaptability to all climates—have been mentioned above. We have also alluded to the irresponsible fecundity with which both species breed at all seasons of the year with a heedlessness of consequences which subjects them to wholesale disaster on the inevitable, occasional failure of the food supply. In this regard, it is only fair to state—in justice to man—that, as far as we can tell, the rat does this of its own free and stupid gluttony, while man has tradition, piety, and the duty of furnishing cannon fodder to contend with, in addition to his lower instincts.—Hans Zinsser, *Rats, Lice and History*, 208

Lechery

But above all, mice and rats for fruitfulness do pass. And therefore I cannot put off the discourse of them any longer: and yet therein I must follow *Aristotle* for mine author, and the report withal of the soldiers that served under *Alexander* the Great. It is said that they engender by licking, without any other kind of copulation: and that one of them hath brought six score at a time: also that in Persia there have been young mice found with young, even in the belly of the old dam.—Pliny, *Pliny's Natural History*, 121

"What happened to the Consul's daughter?" I asked, my curiosity aroused.

"O my! It was terrible. The poor girl is only nineteen, and so pretty too. She happened to be in a state of dishabille when of all things two black rats came in from somewhere and started staring at her. She ran inside, but they followed her. She ran to the dressing room and bolted the door. In a minute the rats appeared at the dressing-room window. As she reached for her dress, she saw the two black brutes ogling and gazing lewdly, fluttering their moustachios. She screamed and fainted. They had to break open the door to reach her."—Ahmed Ali, *Of Rats and Diplomats*, 59

X. would also go to a basement brothel in the Saint-Séverin district.

"Madame," he would say to the proprietress, "do you have any rats today?"

The proprietress would answer as X. expected.

"Yes, Monsieur," she would say, "we have rats."

"Ah . . ."

"But, Madame," X. would continue, "are *these rats* nice ones?"

"Yes, Monsieur, very nice rats."

"Really? but these rats . . . are they big?"

"You'll see, they're enormous rats."

"Because I need huge rats, you understand . . ."

"Ah, Monsieur, giants . . ."

X. would then pounce on an old prostitute who was waiting for him.

—Georges Bataille, *The Impossible: A Story of Rats*, 37

The story of Proust and the rats is circulated to this day, in preposterously elaborated forms, among the inverts of Paris and their foreign visitors. But of its basic truth there can unhappily be no doubt, since it is confirmed by independent witnesses, and still more conclusively by its unmistakable though disguised appearance in his novel. Maurice Sachs heard it from Albert Le Cuziat; Gide and Bernard Fay and Boni de Castellane from

Illustration by Duhamel of the la Fontaine fable "*Le rat et l'huître*" ("The Rat and the Oyster"), nineteenth century.

The rat of course I rate first. He lives in your house without helping you to buy it or build it or repair it or keep the taxes paid; he eats what you eat without helping you raise it or buy it or even haul it into the house; you cannot get rid of him; were he not a cannibal, he would long since have inherited the earth.—William Faulkner, *The Reivers*, 121

"Would you like to see what we do with the rats?"—Proust quoted in George D. Painter, *Proust: The Later Years*, 269

Proust himself; and between the wars it was possible and fashionable to meet the very chauffeur who declared, with a proud and beaming smile: "It was I who used to take the rats to Monsieur Marcel!" The wretched creatures were pierced with hatpins or beaten with sticks, while Proust looked on . . . No doubt his victims represented many things; for rats are among the most powerful, universal and complex symbols in the inferno of the unconscious.—George D. Painter, *Proust: The Later Years*, 269–70

Covetousness

Like the magpie, [the brown rat] steals and hoards small gadgets and coins. In nest chambers in a system of tunnels under a Chelsea tenement, workers recently found an empty lipstick tube, a religious medal, a skate key, a celluloid teething ring, a belt buckle, a shoehorn, a penny, a dime, and three quarters. Paper money is sometimes found. When the Civic Repertory Theatre was torn down, a nest constructed solely of dollar bills, seventeen in all, was discovered in a burrow.—Joseph Mitchell, "The Rats on the Waterfront," 61

Detail from a J.J. Grandville illustration in Scènes de la vie privée et publique des animaux, *1842.*

Eighteenth-century catchpenny print.

Wrath

What rats do when a member of a strange rat clan enters their territory or is put in there by a human experimenter is one of the most horrible and repulsive things which can be observed in animals. The strange rat may run around for minutes on end without having any idea of the terrible fate awaiting it; and the resident rats may continue for an equally long time with their ordinary affairs till finally the stranger comes close enough to one of them for it to get wind of the intruder. The information is transmitted like an electric shock through the resident rat, and at once the whole colony is alarmed by a process of mood transmission which is communicated in the Brown Rat by expression movements but in the House Rat by a sharp, shrill, satanic cry which is taken up by all members of the tribe within earshot.

With their eyes bulging from their sockets, their hair standing on end, the rats set out on the rat hunt. They are so angry that if two of them meet they bite each other.—Konrad Lorenz, *On Aggression*, 161–62

Rat aggression is "evil in the real sense of the word."—Konrad Lorenz, *On Aggression*, 157

Illustration of a rat's incisors from the Century Encyclopedia.

79

ubi erat arca dei. et
... milatuiu. et ideo no...
...mplius tanta pestem
...uit abeustte eua...
...asse aureis. ad
...lacandum ma...
...ust. et arcam
...uasi in plau-
...stro imponentes
...uaccis duabus
...ulos lactantiu...
...us trahebat. pul-
...us earum con-
...lusist ab me pmi-
...erunt. ut uiferet
...quo ueuit. hic in-
...ellectur an deus
...srl. an casus for-
...uicus pestem eis
...ntulisset.

munerum es et
...ualentes sue
philistium arca...

...deram bersabee quam
uiresikas qui metebant triticum in campis sea
cum gaudio susceperunt.

valiter leuite exposuerunt arcam et capsel-
lam cum uasis aureis. super magnum la-
pidem.

vali Bethsamite plausbu et uaccas im-
misso igne comburiu. sacrificium offe-
rentes. et deiuu arca in suu locum reponitur.

9. PLAGUES AND CURES

Rats carry fleas. Fleas can carry plague. If fleas don't have an animal host handy, they live on humans. Both rats and humans can catch the plague. Nowadays we think of plague as a disease of the dark ages, but the truth is we are never far from a plague outbreak. Wherever there are rats and squirrels, there is the chance of plague. Plague has been reported in the western United States: San Francisco grappled with its own outbreak as recently as 1908, and Los Angeles in 1924, according to Arnold Mallis in his *Handbook of Pest Control*.

Philip Ziegler, in his book *The Black Death*, gives a detailed account of opinions and beliefs held by writers and physicians of the fourteenth century. An illuminated manuscript, reproduced in the book, by the artist Aldobrandini of Siena, illustrates his belief that the plague was transmitted by the corrupt fumes of toads, lizards and rats.

In spite of the long history and the devastation of plague around the world, and the fact that rats are as severely affected by plague as humans, no one made the connection until 1894 when two scientists, Professor Kitasato of Japan and Dr Yersin of France, working independently, discovered the plague bacillus. That year marked the arrival of the Third Pandemic in Hong Kong, a vicious occurrence of the plague that started in China in 1855, moved to Hong Kong and then swept west to India. The final connection—the flea as the carrier—was discovered by Paul Louis Simond and described by him in a paper in 1898.

Bubonic plague is the most common form of plague, transmitted by either a bite from a plague-carrying flea or contact with infected dirt or dust on broken skin. The main symptom is inflammation (known as buboes) of the glands. Plague can occur wherever plague fleas and plague rats exist. The mortality rate is 40 to 70 per cent.

PLAGUE VOCABULARY

Quarantine: to isolate the ill or suspected ill. The term came from the Italian practice of detaining travellers for forty days in the fifteenth and sixteenth centuries.
Bacillus: bacteria, specifically rod-shaped and aerobic. The plague bacillus is known as *Pasteurella Pestis.*
Flea: The *Xenopsylla cheopis* is the most efficient plague carrier known, still the most common species of flea in Egypt. *Pulex irritans,* the flea that feeds on humans, is not as efficient.

FACING PAGE: *A page depicting a passage from 1 Samuel. a) Ashdod is smitten with pestilence and a plague of mice/The ark comes to Beth-Shmesh; b) The Levites place the ark and the offering on a great stone/sacrifice of the wain and the cattle. France (probably Paris), c. 1250 C.E. M.638, f21v. By permission of The Pierpont Morgan Library, New York, U.S.A./Art Resource, N.Y.*

Septicemic plague is known as the "Black Death" because of the hemorrhaging that occurs under the skin. Transmission is from the bite of an infected flea, and it almost always results in death. Pneumonic plague occurs after contact with infected dead or dying rodents. It is particularly virulent as it is carried by airborne particles.

Rats carry other diseases besides plague. Most of these diseases are transmitted by handling or eating contaminated food:

Chorio-lepto meningitis (virus): A mild form of meningitis.

Infectious jaundice, aka *Weil's disease*

Hanta (virus): transmission from rat droppings. Can result in death.

Lassa fever (virus, West Africa): transmission by rat sneezes. Can result in death.

Murine typhus fever (southwestern U.S.): transmission by contact with oriental rat flea and rat droppings.

Poliomyelitis (infantile paralysis)

Rat-bite fever: transmission from rat bites. Results in a relapsing fever, especially in children.

Trichinosis: transmission from microscopic worms *(Trichinella spiralis)* through the eating of contaminated food (or undercooked rats!).

—from *Colors* magazine and Arnold Mallis, *Handbook of Pest Control*

Accounts of Plagues

Then said they, What *shall be* the trespass offering which we shall return to him? They answered, Five golden emerods, and five golden mice, *according to* the number of the lords of the Philistines: for one plague *was* on you all, and on your lords.—I Samuel 6:4

The situation worsened in the following days. There were more and more dead vermin in the streets and the scavengers had bigger vanloads every morning. On the fourth day the rats began to come out and die in batches. From basements, cellars and sewers they emerged in long wavering files into the light of day, swayed helplessly, then did a sort of pirouette and fell dead at the feet of the horrified onlookers . . . Some stole forth to die singly in the halls of public offices, in school playgrounds, and even on café terraces. Our townsfolk were amazed to find such busy centres as the Place d'Armes, the boulevards, the Strand dotted with repulsive little corpses.—Albert Camus, *The Plague*, 15

Wherefore were we ordered to kill all the dogs and cats, but because as they were domestic animals, and are apt to run from house to house, and from street to street, so they are capable of carrying the effluvia or infectious streams of bodies infected even in their furs and hair . . .

It is incredible, if their account is to be depended upon, what a prodigious number of those creatures were destroyed. I think they talked of forty thousand dogs, and five times as many cats, few houses being without a cat, some having several, sometimes five or six in a house. All possible endeavours were used, also, to destroy the mice and rats, especially the latter, by laying ratsbane and other poisons for them, and a prodigious multitude were also destroyed.—Daniel Defoe, *Journal of the Plague Year*, 137

Smintheus was a Greek term for a rather ratty variety of mouse, and the association of rats with plague is well known. By contrast, then, the mole appeared as the "blind rat," the denoxified, chthonian permutation of the Apollonian plague animal. Archaeological evidence for this relationship has been found in excavations on Larissa, the acropolis of Argos in the eastern Peloponnesus, where terra-cotta figurines of mice or rats from about 700 B.C. appear with blindfolds or lying on their backs with bellies slit open and eyes bandaged. These objects point to some kind of sacrificial

PLAGUES
First Pandemic: from Africa into Europe (A.D. 541–544) with fourteen successive plagues from A.D. 557–767, including Ireland A.D. 534–680, Constantinople A.D. 540, France A.D. 547, Constantinople A.D. 558, Italy A.D. 591, England A.D. 664.
Second Pandemic: 1347–52 throughout Europe and the Mediterranean, with outbreaks reccurring until 1771.
Third Pandemic: from China to Hong Kong (1855–94) and then on to India, still occurring sporadically today.
—from Duplaix, Shrewsbury, Dols

In 1891 it was possible to say "with some confidence" that the plague was a soil-poison generated out of the products of cadaveric decay.—F. P. Wilson, *The Plague in Shakespeare's London*, 1

FACING PAGE: Memento mori, *c. 1770 by Celebrano Francesco (1729–1814), Italian. Painted wood, cork, clay, cloth, and metal clamps. Courtesy of the National Gallery of Canada, Ottawa.*

Winter settled hard over the Black Sea. The soul of Master Snickup now grew pure—a hagiographical commonplace—as his body grew diseased. He never washed his bed save with tears. The tattered blue cloak had become infested with worms and rotifers,

Which also battened on his holy flesh.

It snew. And on that desolate shale island, since fabled, Master Snickup one day actually looked into the heart of silence, rose and—with a tweak-and-shake of finger and thumb toward the sky—died. Rats performed the exequies.

The moon, suddenly, was o'ercast blood-red in an eclipse. Thunder rumbled. Boding?

III.

A rat flea, black in wing and hackle, flittered out of the shred of blue cloak and flew inland—as if carried along by destiny—toward the Crimean trading port of Kaffa. The infamous date was 1346.—Alexander Theroux, "Master Snickup's Cloak," 142–43

Rats can carry up to seventeen different species of flea at one time.— J. F. D. Shrewsbury, *A History of Bubonic Plague*, 2

ritual involving rats and their sightless permutations.—Jaan Puhvel, "The Mole in Folk Medicine," 33

The first Europeans to catch the plague were early victims of biological warfare. Besieged by Tartars in the Crimean trading city of Caffa, Genovese merchants watched with alarm as the plague-stricken attackers, who were clearly "fatigued, stupefied and amazed" by the pestilence, lobbed their plague dead over the city walls as a parting gesture. Merchants that survived the bacterial bombardment soon fled to their home ports carrying the plague with them.—Andrew Nikiforuk, *The Fourth Horseman*, 45

The pestilence resulted from a corruption occurring in the substance of the air due to heavenly and terrestrial causes. In the earth the causes are brackish water and the many cadavers found in places of battle when the dead are not buried, and land which is water-logged and stagnant from rottenness, vermin, and frogs. As regards the heavenly air, the causes are the many shooting stars and meteorites at the end of the summer and in the autumn, the strong south and east winds in December and January, and when the signs of rain increase in the winter but it does not rain.
—Ibn an-Nafis, a fourteenth-century Egyptian physician quoted in Michael W. Dols, *The Black Death in the Middle East*, 88

In New Guinea in 1943, the official charge for trapping and poisoning rats aboard ships was £0, 10s, 6p for every vessel docked under 50 tons gross. For larger ships the fees increased relative to the numbers of traps set. Fumigation had to be done by the vessel's owners under the supervision of a quarantine officer for a fee of £1, 1s plus expenses. The certificate declaring the ship fumigated cost an extra 10s. To exempt a ship from deratization cost £1, 1s, 0p, but the offical charges sheet does not specify just how one could get a ship exempted. Further charges included disinfecting packages of second-hand clothing and supervision of the scouring of animal hair.—from the *Official Handbook of the Territory of New Guinea*, 483

It is the firm faith of almost all the Europeans living in the East, that Plague is conveyed by the touch of infected substances, and that the deadly atoms especially lurk in all kinds of clothes, and furs: it is held safer, to breathe the same air with a man sick of the Plague, and even to come in contact with his skin, than to be touched by the smallest particle of woollen, or of thread which may have been within the reach of possible infection. If this be a right notion, the spread of the malady must be materially aided by the observance of a custom prevailing amongst the people of Stamboul. It is this; when an Osmanlee dies, one of his dresses is cut up, and a small piece of it is sent to each of his friends, as a memorial of the departed— a fatal present, according to the opinion of the Franks, for it too often forces the living not merely to remember the dead man, but to follow, and bear him company.—A.W. Kinglake, *Eothen*, 22

The medieval house might have been built to specifications approved by a rodent council as eminently suitable for the rat's enjoyment of a healthy and care-free life.—Philip Ziegler, *The Black Death*, 119

In 1897 the surgeon-general of the United States Marine-Hospital Service said, in a paper on plague, "The fact that mortality among rats precedes an outbreak of plague among human beings is explained by Lowson by the fact that rats have their snouts about one inch above the floors of houses and are more liable to inspire plague-infected dust than are human beings."—Geddes Smith, *Plague on Us*, 318

In 1935—not a very bad plague year—the public health commissioner reported the killing in India and Burma of exactly 5,350,003 rats. Rats, to be sure, do not stay massacred: the race is hardy, prolific, and peripatetic.—Geddes Smith, *Plague on Us*, 176

Negroponte had died the day before. When they came to lay out the body, they found the bites: perhaps of some tropical insect? The doctor was vague. "The only such bites I have seen," he said, "were during the plague of Naples when the rats had been at the bodies. They were so bad we had to dust him down with talcum powder before we could let his sister see the body."—Lawrence Durrell, *Balthazar*, 350

CURES
If a Muslim were devout and repeated "the Subduer" over the ill 2142 times, plague would depart. The divine name "the Believer" was considered by some to be the most beneficial during a plague epidemic and should be repeated 136 times a day, but if necessary 299 times a day. Further, it was advisable to put this word into a square and engrave it on a square piece of silver, and the talisman would ward off the evil when it was carried.—Michael W. Dols, *The Black Death in the Middle East*, 128

A plague o' both your houses!—
Zounds, a dog, a rat, a mouse, a cat.
—William Shakespeare, *Romeo and Juliet*, Act III, Scene I

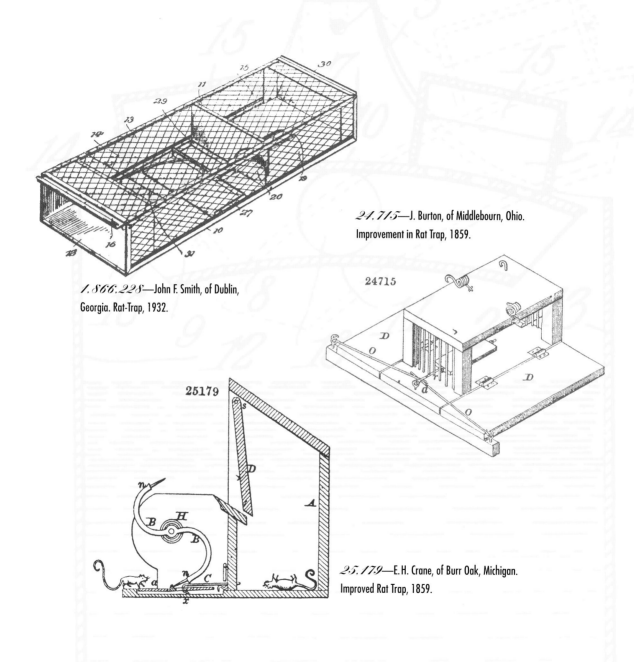

1.866.228—John F. Smith, of Dublin, Georgia. Rat-Trap, 1932.

24.715—J. Burton, of Middlebourn, Ohio. Improvement in Rat Trap, 1859.

24715

25179

25.179—E.H. Crane, of Burr Oak, Michigan. Improved Rat Trap, 1859.

10. TO CATCH A RAT

*34,442—C.R. Morehouse, of
Cardington, Ohio. Improvement in Rat
Traps, 1862.*

The files at patent offices around the world bulge with the plans and promises of hopeful inventors. These creative minds have produced steam engines, cameras, computers and rat traps. And such traps! Traps that break backs, traps that fill up with water, traps that zap with electric current, traps that scoot the rat into a freezer and traps that flip the unsuspecting rodent into a convenient bucket (for later removal to the wilds). People have shot, poisoned, trapped, tricked and beguiled rats out of sight, but only for a while. Rats always seem to come back.

The age-old occupation of rat catcher has now been replaced by the pest-control engineer, and the bounty on rat tails has been superseded by chemical warfare. All to no avail—the rat population is as healthy as ever.

My answer is always the same; I tell them that I prefer rat-catching in Hell to blowing bubbles in Heaven.
—Wyndham Lewis, *Malign Fiesta*, 152

An eighteenth-century woodcut of a rat catcher displaying his booty.

History

The original rat killer, Apollo, has already been introduced as a mythological character. This is the story of the origins of Apollo's name:

Apollo received this derogatory sobriquet from the following incident:— Crinis, one of his priests, having neglected his official duties, Apollo sent against him a swarm of rats; but the priest, seeing the invaders coming, repented and obtained forgiveness of the god, who annihilated the swarms which he had sent with his far-darting arrows. For this redoubtable exploit the sun-god received the appellation of Apollo the Rat-killer.—*Brewer's Dictionary of Phrase & Fable*, 1040

We never allow rats to be poisoned in our dwelling, they are so liable to die between the walls and produce much annoyance.—*Dr Chase's Third, Last and Complete Receipt Book*, 5

Although poison has long been considered the method of choice for controlling rats, there are other methods, such as the reading of the Gospel of St John

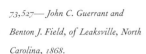

from three corners of a house. The rats should escape from the fourth. A corner chosen wisely could lead them to the house of a despised or rich neighbour.

Rats can also be driven off with the help of other rats. It is not an easy matter to catch a rat and to tie a bell around it, but at least it is not nearly as vicious as catching a rat and setting it alight, an episode we may read about in *I, Jan Cremer*. In that book, Jan Cremer tells us that all the rats on board a ship dived into the water after one of them had been doused in petrol and set ablaze.—Martin Hart, *Rats*, 142

73,527— John C. Guerrant and Benton J. Field, of Leaksville, North Carolina, 1868.

Trapping Rats

"[We take] a shingle smeared on one side with a thick, strong, black glue. We developed this glue twenty-five years ago and it's probably the stickiest stuff known to man . . . We place them on rat runs—the paths rats customarily travel on—and that's where skill comes in; you have to be an expert to locate the rat runs. We lay bait around the boards. If any part of the animal touches a board, he's done for. When he tries to pull away, he gets himself firmly caught in the glue. The more he struggles, the more firmly he's caught. Next morning the rat, glueboard and all, is picked up with tongs and burned. We used to bait with ground beef, canned salmon, and cheese, but we did some experimenting with many other foods and discovered that peanut butter is an extremely effective rat bait."—quoted in Joseph Mitchell, "The Rats on the Waterfront," 58

968,966—Carl Miller, of College Springs, Iowa. Rat or Mouse Trap, 1910.

The *Globe and Mail* described a rat trap called the Ratapault that heaves its victims as far as 15 metres into a waiting bucket. The trap, invented by a company in California, is a small box armed with an infrared trip light and a catapult device. It apparently does not kill the animal.—from the *Globe and Mail*, February 19, 1992

690,291—Edward G. Hummell, of Lancaster, New York. Mouse or Rat Trap, 1901.

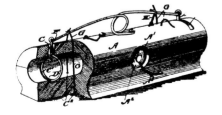

Difficulties

With regards to general intelligence, every one knows the extraordinary wariness of rats in relation to traps, which is only equalled in the animal kingdom by that of the fox and the wolverine. It has frequently been regarded as a wonderful display of intelligence on the part of rats that while gnawing through the woodwork of a ship, they always stop before they completely perforate the side; but . . . this is probably due to their distaste of the salt water.—George J. Romanes, *Animal Intelligence*, 361

Trap Types

CURIOSITY SUCKS LIFE OUT OF RATS

The Ikari corporation of Japan has developed a rat trap guaranteed not only to attract the animal but also to grab it, send it flying, freeze it and keep it in storage until an appropriate time comes to dispose of it. The trap is made of long tubes, and heat sensors warn it to arm itself at the approach of a rat or mouse. If the animal enters through one of the many small holes along the sides of the tube, the doors slam shut, and fans blow powerful blasts of air that push the rat to a freezer compartment at the end of the tube. Once the animal is frozen, the contraption resets itself and the whole thing starts over again.—from the *Globe and Mail*, January 7, 1995

704,576—John T. Prior, of Priors, Georgia. Rat-Killer, 1902.

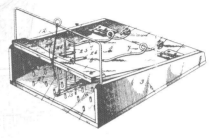

704,910—Peter Olaffsen, of Tacoma, Washington. Rat-Trap, 1902.

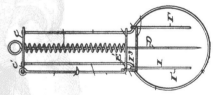

767,220—Charles F. Graeber, of Lytton, Iowa. Rat-Trap, 1903. In case there's any question, the spring-loaded spike in the centre really is intended to impale the animal.

Un Gueux grotesque. *Rat catcher by Jean-George Van Vliet, Dutch, 1836.*

Rat Trappers

In 1768 Princess Amelia's official rat catcher observed that brown rats always got the better of the smaller black rats:

> As a proof of which I was once exercising my employment at a gentleman's house, and when the night came that I appointed to catch, I set all my traps going as usual, and in the lower part of the house in the cellars I caught the Norway rats, but in the upper part of the house I took nothing but black rats. I then put them together into a great cage to keep them alive till the morning, that the gentleman might see them, when the Norway rats killed the black rats immediately and devoured them in my presence.—Graham Twigg, *The Brown Rat*, 23

The Persian and Raoul could retreat no farther and flattened themselves against the wall, not knowing what was going to happen because of that incomprehensible head of fire, and especially now, because of the more intense, swarming, living, "numerous" sound, for the sound was certainly made up of hundreds of little sounds that moved in the darkness, under the fiery face . . .

And the two companions, flat against the wall, felt their hair stand on end with horror, for they now knew what the thousand noises meant. They came in a troop, hustled along in the shadow by innumerable little hurried waves, swifter than the waves that rush over the sands at high tide, little night-waves, foaming under the moon, under the fiery head that was like a moon. And the little waves passed between their legs, climbing up their legs, irresistible, and Raoul and the Persian could no longer restrain their cries of horror, dismay and pain. Nor could they continue to hold their hands at the level of their eyes: their hands went down to their legs to push back the waves, which were full of little legs and nails and claws and teeth.

Yes, Raoul and the Persian were ready to faint, like Pampin the fireman. But the head of fire turned round in answer to their cries, and spoke to them:

"Don't move! Don't move! . . . Whatever you do, don't come after me! . . . I am the rat-catcher! . . . Let me pass, with my rats! . . ."

And the head of fire disappeared, vanished in the darkness, while the passage in front of it lit up, as the result of the change which the rat-catcher had made in his dark lantern. Before, so as not to scare the rats in front of him, he had turned his dark lantern on himself, lighting up his own head; now, to hasten their flight, he lit the dark space in front of him. And he jumped along, dragging with him the waves of scratching rats, all the thousand sounds.—Gaston Leroux, *The Phantom of the Opera*, 174–75

Poisons

It is at all times difficult to get rid of these dirty, noisy [rats], for they soon learn to keep out of the way of traps, and if they are poisoned they revenge their fate by dying behind a wainscot or under a plank of the floor, and make the room uninhabitable. There are, however, two ways recommended to attain the desired object.

Place a saucer containing meal in a room frequented by rats, letting them have free access to it for several days. They will then come to it in great force. When they have thus been accustomed to feed there regularly,

The Rat-Killer, 1632, etching by Rembrandt. Copyright British Museum. Used by permission.

The Goodwill Exterminators have a new exhibit: among the pickled bugs and childishly hand-lettered signs, a jar of milk-white shrimps with tails, labeled "Day-old baby Rats, caught in a Vokswagon [sic] on Perry Street by Leon."—Julie Hayden, "Day-Old Baby Rats," 30

Rat-Catchers motto: By the cat you put rats to flight. If you drive away little thieves by great ones, it is utter folly. Look at me; provided only a little coin is forthcoming, I will put both rats and cats to flight.—Chambers Book of Days, Vol. 2, 104

Ichneumons [see below] also known as "the Pharoah's cat" are frequently tamed, and, when made inmates of houses, answer the purpose of cats, clearing the residence of rats and mice with great rapidity. It is difficult, however, to prevent them from appropriating such things as eggs, poultry, pigeons, and the like, on which account their services are for the most part dispensed with.—George Rawlinson, History of Ancient Egypt, 68–69

mix a quantity of jalap* with the meal, and put it in the accustomed place. This will give them such internal tortures that they will not come near the place again.

The second plan is to use the same precautions, but to mix phosphorus with the meal and make it into a ball. The phosphorus is said not to kill the rats, but to afflict them with such a parching thirst that they rush to the nearest water and die there. By this method the danger of their dying in the house is avoided.

I have not proved either of these plans experimentally, but offer them for the benefit of those who are afflicted by the rat pest.—Rev. J. G. Wood, *The Boy's Own Book of Natural History*, 74–75

*Jalap is a powdered drug from the tuberous root of the *Exogonium purga* plant (related to the morning glory) of Mexico. It has purgative properties.

"Abel's rat-poisoning in the garage," said Paris. "They've all gone out to see he doesn't give himself a lethal dose of prussic acid.". . .

"What form of cyanide has Abel got hold of?" Watchman asked.

"Eh?" said Parish vaguely. "Oh, let's see now. I fetched it for him from Illington. The chemist hadn't got any of the stock rat-banes, but he poked round and found this stuff. I think he called it Scheele's acid."

"Good God!"

"What? Yes, that was it—Scheele's acid. And then he said he thought the fumes of Scheele's acid mightn't be strong enough, so he gingered it up a bit."

"With what, in the name of all the Borgias?"

"Well—with prussic acid, I imagine."

"You imagine! You imagine!"—Ngaio Marsh, *Death at the Bar*, 18

Faust

A Rat in a cellar had his nest
His skin could scarce be smoother;
And his paunch, from feasting on the best,
Was fit for Doctor Luther.

The cook with poison strewed the spot,
And soon he found the place as hot
　　As if love had scorched his liver!
—Goethe, *Faust*, Part I, 123–24

Rat Poison Sandwich

Dr Chase wisely suggests keeping this one away from children:

First spread some slices of bread lightly with butter; then sprinkle on rather freely of the arsenic, and over this with a little sugar, and with a case-knife press the sugar and arsenic well into the butter, so they will not fall off. Now, cut the slices of bread into squares of half an inch or so, and drop into the rat-holes, out of the way of children, chickens, and other animals which you do not wish to kill.—*Dr Chase's Third, Last and Complete Receipt Book*, 584

Impaling

Another dependable method of rat control from Dr Chase:

A German paper gives the following plan . . . "Having first for some days placed pieces of cheese in a part of the premises, so as to induce the rats to come in great numbers to their accustomed feeding-place, a piece of cheese is fixed on a fish-hook about a foot above the floor. One rat leaps at this, and of course remains suspended. Hereat all the other rats take sudden flight, and at once quit the house in a body."

Remarks.—Possibly our Yankee rats may be too smart for this, but it would make some amusement for the boys to try it.—*Dr Chase's Third, Last and Complete Receipt Book*, 584

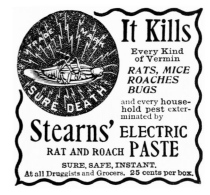

Little Johnny and the other rats
Ate all the Tuff-on-Ratz
Father said, as mother cried
Never mind, they'll die outside.
—children's rhyme quoted in Arnold Mallis, *Handbook of Pest Control*, 71

Logo for rat poison, 1931, Paris. Henri & Antoine Collet.

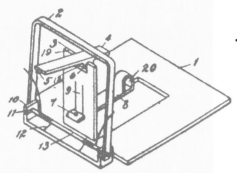

867,163—Samuel Shreffler, of Joliet, Illinois, for the M.A. Felman and Co. Rat and Mouse Trap, 1907.

"You see if I were in charge of the operations, I would finish off the whole race of rodents in one sweeping action, even though I had to employ an army of a hundred million."

"What form would that take? It sounds exciting. Not for nothing have you been a General."

"I shall dig up the fields and farms and mow the running rats down with Sherman tanks."—Ahmed Ali, *Of Rats and Diplomats*, 68

From an advertisement for a Victorian rat trap.

Miscellaneous

In the morning there was a rat leg in the trap, but no rat—just some blood sprayed around. Jimmy said the spring-loaded trap bar had probably broke the rat's leg and the busted bone went through the meat and skin so the rat chewed off the rest and hopped away. "Bugger's in the wall," he roared, "with a Band-aid on his stump, gnawin' a kindlin' stick with his teeth, tryin' to make hisself a pair a' crutches!"—Anne Cameron, *Wedding Cakes, Rats and Rodeo Queens*, 61

The city of Paris has two rat control units, both created in the early 1920s: the Service de lutte contre les rongeurs (Service of the Battle Against the Rats), part of the Préfecture de Police, controlling rats on private property, and the Section de lutte contre les rongeurs, which looks after "public rats." M. Roland Vétil, Chef de service for the latter, noted that the word *lutte* in these instances didn't imply destruction, that they recognized the role that rats play in our society.

"It would be a mistake to eradicate them. But unfortunately they have a bad reputation and people don't like to see them. We try to manage their population so that visitors to Paris don't come across any."

He added, when asked how many rats lived in Paris, "I would love to know how many there are. The fact is we have no idea!" Jean-Paul Lemercier, Technical Assistant to the Service, when asked the same question, replied, "How can you count them when they all look the same?" He also commented:

"People who call us often overestimate the size of the rat. Between the time they see it and the time they get to the phone, they seem to fantasize about it. It soon becomes as large as a kangaroo!"

The Service makes about 11,599 visits a year and the Section about 5300.
—interview by Françoise Giovannangeli with Roland Vétil and Jean-Paul Lemercier

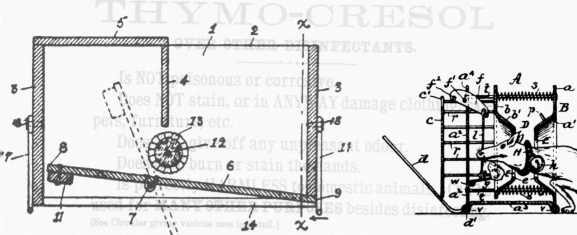

8.30.009—Alsom E. Salisbury, of Toledo, Ohio. Rat Trap, 1906. A "bait-rod" is suspended from the top of the box. It is intended to hold an ear of corn: "said rod being adapted to be inserted lengthwise through an ear of corn and revolubly support the ear, and means to support the box over water in an open-top vessel."

8.83.611—Joseph Barad and Edward E. Markoff, of Providence, Rhode Island. Device Employed for Exterminating Rats, Mice, and Other Animals, 1908. This device has a spring-pressed frame outfitted with an elastic collar that is placed to ensnare the animal around the neck.

26495

26.495—Simson S. Henderson, of Oxford, Ohio. Improved Rat Trap, 1859. The inventor says: "In the operation of this trap I put, in the first place, bait on bait wire d, the triggers being self setting. I now take hold of the crank and turn until the springs are almost brought down to the spools H. If now a rat pull on the bait attached to wire d, detent b will be discharged from dog a, which being freed permits striker G to fly round rapidly and strike the rat with force, instantly killing it and throwing it out of the way."

8.95.473—Thomas Knight, of Atlanta, Georgia. Rat-Trap, 1908

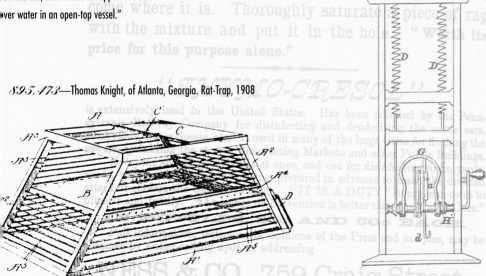

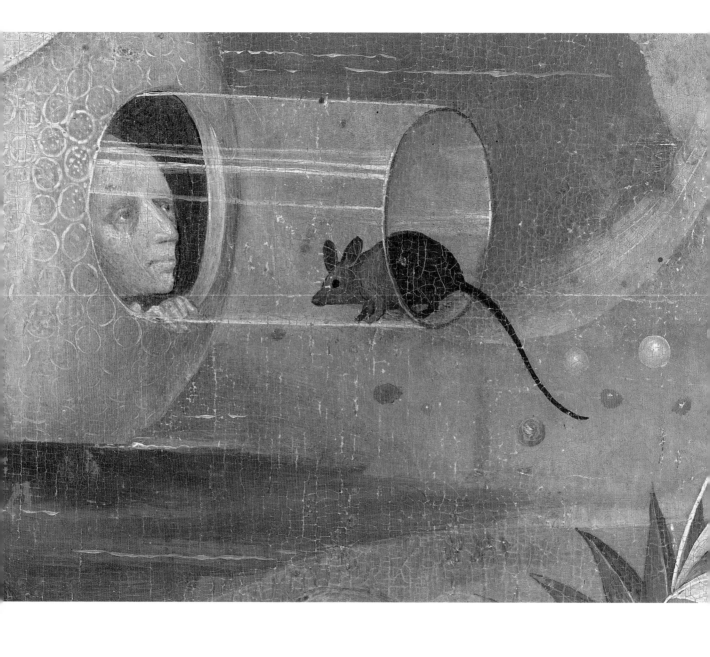

11. RATS AND MAN

It would be an understatement to say that humans and rats have shared an existence marked by mutual terror, distrust and loathing. Rats eat our garbage, they live in our buildings and they sail on our boats. We, in turn, either poison or trap them or stand cowering in their presence. Statistics proclaim that for every human being on this earth, there is a rat. And rats are the constant worry of health departments around the world. A rat population out of control could mean the spread of more disease, the destruction of even more crops and food-stuffs and a panic that comes from confrontation with a generally poorly under-stood adversary. Yet much of what we know of ourselves has come from the millions of studies scientists have made of rats. Physical and behavioral reac-tions to drugs or to stress, to removal of body parts, to crowding or isolation, have been studied in comparison to humans. But watching a white rat in a lab-oratory cage is different from confronting a brown rat sitting in a garbage can. When faced with such a situation, we don't think of B. F. Skinner's maze exper-iments or dissections of rat pituitary glands. We ask ourselves what we're going to do now: run, hide or scream?

Rats and humans have coexisted through feast and famine, war and peace. Rats are in our religions and in our dreams and, in spite of our never-ending quest for the means to rid ourselves of them, we can't resist giving them human qualities.

> "Rats are smart. Some say they're as smart as people."
> "If that was only how smart they were they'd'a died out long ago."
> —Anne Cameron, *Wedding Cakes, Rats and Rodeo Queens*, 82

I think we are in rats' alley
Where the dead men lost their bones
—T.S. Eliot, *The Waste Land*, 65

Neither rat nor man has achieved social, commercial, or economic stability. This has been, either perfectly or to some extent, achieved by ants and by bees . . . Man and the rat are merely, so far, the most successful animals of prey. They are utterly destructive of other forms of life. Neither of them is of the slightest earthly use to any other species of living things.—Hans Zinsser, *Rats, Lice and History*, 208

FACING PAGE: *Detail*, The Solemn Man and the Rat, *from the painting* The Garden of Earthly Delights (Hell). *Hieronymus Bosch.* © *Museo del Prado, Madrid, all rights reserved. Used by permission.*

PNEU VÉLO LEFORT

Etabl.ᵗˢ LEFORT. ROMANS (Drôme)

Pneu Vélo Lefort poster by Capiello, from 100 ans d'affiches du cycle. *Bibliothèque Nationale, Paris.*

Playthings

"Do you love rats?"

"No! I hate them!"

"Well, I do, too—*live* ones. But I mean dead ones, to swing round your head with a string."

"No, I don't care for rats much, anyway. What I like is chewing-gum."—Tom Sawyer and Becky Thatcher in Mark Twain's *The Adventures of Tom Sawyer*, 62

Uneasy Coexistence

Some appetite waits and lurks in the world, you remark; it is some great hunger, insect and rodent and decay hunger. This seems suddenly to be a law of the universe. Insect, mold, rat, rust, death—all wait for and get the human plunder in the end, to carry the carrion away.—William Goyen, *The House of Breath*, 55

We would gladly, figuratively speaking, have held the basin for his overflow, we the foot soldiers of his deliriums, we the model of his terrors. That's why man made word pictures of us. He feared ratbite fever, he cursed rats' nests and rat races . . . Even more than spiders we disgusted him . . . Because our tails were naked and unreasonably long, they were especially repugnant to him; we were the embodiment of disgust. Even in books that celebrated self-revulsion as specific to human existence, we would be read between the lines; for when man felt disgust for man, as he had seen fit to do from time immemorial, it was we once again who helped him to find names for it; whenever he had his enemy, his many enemies, in his sights, he would cry: You rat! You rats!—Günter Grass, *The Rat*, 86

Something was dropping out of a tree, turning over and over as it fell. A miniature body. It hit the parking lot and went still.

That's when I felt a hostile animal presence. I looked straight out through the windshield. Clinging to the wipers was a yellow-eyed rat.

Even through the glass, I could smell its bad breath . . . I turned the ignition key one click forward and threw on the windshield wipers. Get out of my sight, Rat. But Rat clung to the rubber blade with all four claws. It rode back and forth across the glass, its back feet scratching furiously at the windshield, raising an intolerable sound.

I put the wipers on high. Take that, Rat. But Rat rode it out, teeth and claws sunk into the wipers blade. It was like a roller coaster for rats. You could tell Rat was trying to figure out what to do in a situation like this. It was his first time he was faced with such a thing.

That makes two of us, Rat. Should we talk?

I bailed out of the car. You can keep it, Rat, the papers are in the glove compartment.—David Homel, *Rat Palms*, 224–25

"Landlord, huh?" he says . . . "You tell him there is *bugs* in here. Bugs, and *rats*. You tell him that. You tell him we want them bugs and rats out, we ain't payin' no *rent*. Shit. They're not payin' the rent now."

"Rats?" Proctor said.

"Yeah," Fein said, "rats. Course I've got rats in there. I got rats that walk on two legs. Why the hell wouldn't I have the rats that walk on four?"—George V. Higgins, *The Rat on Fire*, 44

Men as Rats

The race of poets themselves have turned into subterranean rats scuttling along the City's hidden sewers and obscure margins, as obsolete as the courtesans who once served as their umbilical cords . . . Besides, aren't poets a kind of rat species today, endlessly scuttling along hidden sewage pipes and through underground grottoes, embarrassing and boring entities whose

PSYCHOLOGY

That evening, I went to see my psychoanalyst. "So what about rats—what does it mean if you're afraid of rats?" I asked impatiently.

"Nothing," he said calmly. "Rats are not symbolic of anything. They are a fact. They must just be coped with."
—"The Big Boys" from *The New Yorker*, 30

If there is one thing I hate more than another it is a rat running over me in the darkness. However, I had the satisfaction of catching one of them a good punch that sent him flying.—George Orwell, *Down and Out in Paris and London*, 83

MUSIC

The Irish rock-and-roll group, The Boomtown Rats (with Bob Geldof), were named after a gang in Woody Guthrie's song *Bound for Glory*. They were formed in 1975 and broke up in 1986.—Patricia Romanowski, *The New Rolling Stone Encyclopedia of Rock & Roll*

That'll teach a lesson
To the' boom town rats!
—Woody Guthrie, *Bound for Glory*, 124

A. himself has the dash and character of a rat—all the more alarming because one doesn't know where he comes from nor where he makes off to.—Georges Bataille, *The Impossible: A Story of Rats*, 38

These curious specimens (known as "Broetteig") are made of gum tragacanth, sugar and meal, and after hardening in moulds are painted. Made throughout the seventeenth and eighteenth century, their heyday was in the nineteenth, when they were made by every pastry-cook in Swabia . . . the mad Peter III of Russia must have been addicted to them, as he once ordered a rat which had eaten two of these delicacies to be sentenced to death according to martial law!—John G. Garratt, *Model Soldiers: A Collector's Guide*, 118–19

Collector card #31: Brown rat and young, *from John Player and Sons tobacco company.*

metrical effusions give rise only to perfectly oval yawns? The poet has become a rat, both spiritually and—more importantly—physically. The problem with rats is that they breed.—Lawrence Osborne, *Paris Dreambook*, 182

I liked him at once. He was about my age, in the early twenties, scrawny, with a thin, mobile face deeply scorched by the sun. He had that brightness of eye and the quick, slightly sardonic turn to his mouth that I associated with faces in the coffee-houses of universities in Delhi and Calcutta; he seemed to belong to a world of late-night rehearsals and black coffee and lecture rooms, even though, in fact, unlike most people in the village, he was completely illiterate. Later I learned that he was called the Rat—Khamees the Rat—because he was said to gnaw away at things with his tongue, like a rat did with its teeth.—Amitav Ghosh, "The Imam and the Indian," *Granta Travel*, 184

The Rat

As often as he let himself be seen
We pitied him, or scorned him, or deplored
The inscrutable profusion of the Lord
Who shaped as one of us a thing so mean—
Who made him human when he might have been
A rat, and so been wholly in accord
With any other creature we abhorred
As always useless and not always clean
—Edward Arlington Robinson, "The Rat," 179

The Law

Chambers Book of Days describes trials that were conducted against various wild animals such as rats, locusts and caterpillars. The trials depended upon the belief that the church had been granted full power to excommunicate animals and humans alike. Summonses were served, read at the place where the animals gathered, and the animals were expected to obey and show up in court. In order to avoid mistakes, the summons contained a description of the accused animal. In one particular trial held in France, in the diocese of Autun, proceedings dragged on from 1445 until well after 1487. Chambers comments that all concerned would have been "pretty well fleeced" by the expenses of the trial:

> The defendants were described as dirty animals in the form of rats, of a greyish colour, living in holes. This trial is famous in the annals of French law, for it was at it that Chassanee, the celebrated jurisconsult . . . won his first laurels. The rats not appearing on the first citation, Chassanee, their counsel, argued that the summons was of a too local and individual character; that, as all the rats in the diocese were interested, all the rats should be summoned, in all parts of the diocese. This plea being admitted, the curate of every parish in the diocese was instructed to summon every rat for a future date. The day arriving, but no rats, Chassanee said that, as all his clients were summoned, including young and old, sick and healthy, great preparations had to be made, and certain arrangements carried into effect, and therefore he begged for an extension of time. This also being granted, another day was appointed, and no rats appearing, Chassanee objected to the legality of the summons, under certain circumstances. A summons from that court, he argued, implied full protection to the parties summoned, both on their way to it and on their return home; but his clients, the rats, though most anxious to appear in obedience to the court, did not dare to stir out of their holes on account of the number of evil-disposed cats kept by the plaintiffs. Let the latter, he continued, enter into bonds, under heavy pecuniary penalties, that their cats shall not molest my clients, and the summons will be at once obeyed. The court acknowledged the validity of this plea; but, the plaintiffs declining to be bound over for the good behaviour of their cats, the period for the rats' attendance was adjourned *sine die*; and thus, Chassanee gaining his cause, laid the foundation of his future fame.—*Chambers Book of Days*, Vol. 1, 127–28

[Rats] spend most of their lives in a state of extreme anxiety, the black rats dreading the brown and both species dreading human beings. Away from their nests, they are usually on the edge of hysteria.—Joseph Mitchell, "The Rats on the Waterfront," 54–55

The cat came back again, the one that had frightened her before, and she watched its slow, cautious circuitous return to the place from which they had routed it . . .

You can kill a rat, she found herself addressing it enviously in her mind, and they praise you for it. And your kind of rat only bites, they don't suck blood.—Cornell Woolrich, *I Married a Dead Man*, 204

S. GERTRVDIS VIRGO.
Nivellis Abbatissa Canoniss: Reg: S. August:
R.^{de} D^{na} Priorissa Canoniss.arum.Reg. S. Augustini
Ioanna Blitterswyck Bruxellis in Iericho. DD.C.Q.

Like man—the rat is individualistic until it needs help. That is, it fights bravely alone against weaker rivals, for food or for love; but it knows how to organize armies and fight in hordes when necessary.—Hans Zinsser, *Rats, Lice and History*, 196–97

Religion

I leaned over to the good priest and said: "Has it not happened to you, after consecration to remain in adoration, motionless, as if speechless, for a considerable time?"

"Yes," he answered, sobbing, "but what does this have to do with God's disappearance?"

My soul filled with sadness . . . I told him, "The rats have undoubtedly taken and eaten God!"

"What are you saying?" he answered. "God taken and eaten by rats!"

"Yes," I replied, "I no longer have any doubt about it!"

—Charles Chiniquy, *Le Bon Dieu de Rome mangé par les rats*

Several saints are associated with rats. The first one, Saint Fina, also known as Saint Serafina, lived during the thirteenth century in a small town in Tuscany. Rats have a rather unfortunate association with Saint Fina: ill for most of her brief life, she made the most of her suffering, and towards the end lay on a hard board waiting for death. Rats attacked her, but she was too ill to stop them. Since then, when represented in art, she is shown in association with the rat.

Sainte Gertrude de Nivelles, Bibliothèque Nationale, Paris.

Sainte Gertrude de Nivelles lived in Belgium during the seventh century. Immediately after her death, a number of miracles were attributed to her devotional powers, including the suppressing of fevers, the protection of travellers and, most of all, making rats and mice go away. She, like Saint Fina, is shown with rats. It is said that both the consecrated earth from the cemetery where she is buried and the holy water from the crypt of the church have the power to drive away rats.—from Michel Dansel, *Nos frères les rats*, 112–13

Rats and Garbage

For three days now the garbage men's strike has been strewing its splendors along every street in Roanne. In honor of what festival, one wonders, have these writhing, multicolored shrines been erected before every house, rising sometimes as high as the second-floor windows, so that pedestrians walk in a kind of trench between the building and a picturesque barricade. It is a new kind of Corpus Christi, Corpus Ganesh, the trunked idol whose totem is the rat. Because, of course, the rats from the depots, deprived of fresh food, have invaded the town and their black hordes are spreading panic in the side streets at night.—Michel Tournier, *Gemini*, 151

Rats and Politics

"Have you read, my dear, the mad doctor's theory about birth control among rats?"

"Wasn't that funny, Anne darling? Imagine anyone suggesting such a thing! I never heard of birth control among rats! They must destroy the whole lot of them."

"What angered me was the suggestion that women should take the pills too."

"That is what I say. Women and rats have been lumped together. That's outrageous, and an insult to womankind! I suggested to my husband that he should protest to the Foreign Office."—Ahmed Ali, *Of Rats and Diplomats*, 63

In that golden century of faith not only sinful human beings but all mischievous animals, such as rats, ravens, wild boars, worms, tape-worms and fleas were subject to the anathemas of the church if they so much as dared to eat green vegetables or disturb the sleep of the faithful.—Lawrence Durrell, *Pope Joan*, 145

When the ship was moored at Bermuda, alongside the wharf in the dockyard, boards were placed on all the mooring chains as a fence against rats. Rats nevertheless appeared in the ship, and were all curiously enough of the old species, the Black Rat (*Mus rattus*). One night, as we were sitting at whist, Mr. J. Hynes, the Assistant Paymaster, suddenly started up with a yell, and danced about as if gone mad, clutching one of his legs with both hands. A rat had mistaken his trousers for a pipe or wind-sail, and had gone up.—H.N. Moseley, *Notes by a Naturalist on the Challenger*, 594

They are the government, these
    marsh-brained rats
Who give protection from outsider cats
—Alan Sillitoe, *The Rats and Other Poems*, Part I, II

Gustave Doré illustration of the la
Fontaine fable "The War of the Rats
and the Weasels."

FACING PAGE: *This bronze and
brass set of armour for a rat is
based on a fifteenth-century
design.* Maximillian Rat, *1993, by
Jeff de Boer. Photograph by Jason
Stang. Courtesy of Jeff de Boer.*

Rats and War

The rats here are particularly repulsive, they are so fat—the kind we call corpse-rats. They have shocking, evil, naked faces, and it is nauseating to see their long, nude tails.

They seem to be mighty hungry. Almost every man has had his bread gnawed. Kropp wrapped his in his waterproof sheet and put it under his head, but he cannot sleep because they run over his face to get at it. Detering meant to outwit them: he fastened a thin wire to the roof and suspended his bread from it. During the night when he switched on his pocket-torch he saw the wire swinging to and fro. On the bread was riding a fat rat.—Erich Maria Remarque, *All Quiet on the Western Front*, 69

Railroaded (1947), a film noir directed by Anthony Mann:
"You know, there are only two kinds of animals that make war on their own kind—rats and men. And men are supposed to be able to think."
—coroner (bit player) to police technician (bit player)

A nightmarish battle scene took place in Manitoba between giant rats and the Canadian Forces, who thought flamethrowers would annihilate the enemy:
The Canadians could hardly see through the inferno, and the weapons were stopped a short time later in order that Sterling could judge the result of his attack—and he and his men saw! Not one of the damned rats had been stopped dead, turned into ashes. Not one!—Sam Spiller, "The Great Plague of Bronston," 120

ABOVE: *Eighteenth-century catch-penny print of a rat feast, from the firm of Carver and Bowles.*

BELOW: *Nineteenth-century children's nursery rhyme "Pretty John Watts."*

Pretty John Watts,
   We are troubled with rats,
Will you drive them out of the house?
   We have mice too in plenty,
   That feast in the pantry,
But let them stay and nibble away,
What harm in a little brown mouse?

———◦⟨▦▦▦⟩◦———

Shake a leg, wag a leg, when will you gang?
At midsummer, mother, when the days are lang.

Rat Food

A rat is unimpressed by talk of a just peace, he recognizes no flag and his ideology is food. Food! Food!—Gilbert Sorrentino, *Splendide-Hôtel*, 31

Rat Jelly

See the rat in the jelly
Steaming dirty hair
frozen, bring it out on a glass tray
split the pie four ways and eat
I took great care cooking this treat for you
and tho it looks good to yuh
and tho it smells of the Westinghouse still
and tastes of exotic fish or
maybe the expensive arse of a cow
I want you to know it's rat
Steamy dirty hair and still alive

(Caught him last sunday
thinking of the fridge, thinking of you.
—Michael Ondaatje, "Rat Jelly"

The Laboratory Rat

He went into his bedroom and came back a moment later, coatless, his sleeves rolled up. He took the rats off the shelves one by one and weighed them in turn on a scale. The rats knew him. Julio played with them, opening their mouths with his index finger bent to feel their long teeth: they never bit him. He also prepared their food, a white paste which he dried in the sun; after cutting it in equal pieces, he distributed it among the various shelves. This food had a smell which clung to the skin with an insidious persistence, the famous "smell of rat." In vain Julio sprinkled his arms with eau de cologne after washing them in the single jet of the sink; as soon as he entered the dining room, my father—on smelling the eau de cologne—prophesied that bubonic plague would imminently wreak havoc in the family. Julio let him talk. Once, however, he condescended to reply:

"White rats are not carriers of bubonic plague; besides, what you claim to smell is not the rats but the food for the rats, food, I should add in passing, which is quite a bit more hygienic than our own: cornstarch, casein, salt, cod liver oil, and brewer's yeast. I see that you don't look too well; you should try that diet yourself."—José Bianco, *The Rats*, 52–53

In the colony I'm known as Doctor Rat. Having been part of this laboratory so long and having studied so carefully, it's only right I be given some mark of distinction other than the tattoo on the inside of my ear, a mark that all the other rats have too. Some of them have tattoos and V-shaped wedges cut out of their ears. Some even have three or four wedges cut of their ears, but that doesn't mean they are as learned as I. It simply means they have had the liver removed (one wedge), the liver and pituitary gland removed (two wedges), liver, pituitary and pineal glands removed (three wedges), and so forth. After they remove your heart, no more wedges are needed, ha ha!—William Kotzwinkle, *Doctor Rat*, 3

I am a rat named Crocus: sex, male: . . . profession, student of human nature and therefore, of course, of human history . . . My family has . . . been called "Skinner's rats", by way of a joke, you understand. It was, I believe, one of these forebears of mine who made the witticism that he had trained Dr Skinner so well that whenever he pressed a certain bar in his prison Dr Skinner fed him.—Constantine Fitzgibbon, *The Rat Report*

> This is the house that Jack built.
> This is the malt
> That lay in the house that Jack built.
>
>
>
> This is the rat,
> That ate the malt,
> That lay in the house that Jack built.
>
> This is the cat,
> That kill'd the rat,
> That ate the malt,
> That lay in the house that Jack built.

Children's nursery rhyme "The House that Jack Built" from the children's book Journeys Through Bookland, *illustrated by Lucille Enders.*

Meg found her sister eating apples and crying over the *Heir of Redclyffe*, wrapped up in a comforter on an old three-legged sofa by the sunny window. This was Jo's favorite refuge, and here she loved to retire with a half a dozen russets and a nice book, to enjoy the quiet and the society of a pet rat who lived near by and didn't mind her a particle. As Meg appeared, Scrabble whisked into his hole.

—Louisa May Alcott, *Little Women*, 25

Pet Rats

It was just that PatsyRatsy wasn't white. She hadn't been inbred to albinism, she wasn't like those poor things they called dancing mice and sold for five dollars each, which were the product of an inbred genetic flaw similar to cerebral palsy—not dancing at all, merely unable to control their twitching muscles and minor epileptic seizures. If you could give houseroom to a misbred mouse as apt as not to fling itself into the air and come down in your cup of tea, why not a shiny, bright-eyed and friendly rat who was probably twice as smart as any poodle who ever pranced on the end of a leash? But all you had to do was look at PatsyRatsy and every horror story you'd every heard leapt up on stage and started to tap dance. PatsyRatsy wasn't exotic, she was *Rattus rattus*.—Anne Cameron, *Wedding Cakes, Rats and Rodeo Queens*, 119

Across [the] symbolic bars separating two worlds, the open road and the castle, the poor child was showing his own toy to the rich child who was greedily inspecting it like a rare and unknown object. Now, that toy, which the little scum was poking, turning, and shaking in its grated box, was a living rat! His parents, probably to save money, had extracted the toy from life itself.—Charles Baudelaire, "The Pauper's Toy," *Parisian Prowler*, 40–41

J.J. Grandville illustration from his book Scènes de la vie privée et publique des animaux, *1842.*

Illustration by Alice Wheaton-Adams from Tom Tucker and Little Bo-Peep.

Nursery Rats

There was a little bachelor, who lived all by himself,
And all the bread and cheese he had he put upon a shelf,
The rats and the mice they led him such a life,
He was forced to go to London to buy him a wife.

—Thomas Hood, with illustrations by Alice Wheaton-Adams,

Tom Tucker and Little Bo-Peep, 31

There was a rat,
For want of stairs,
Went down a rope
To say his prayers.

—traditional children's nursery rhyme

Illustration by Herbert N. Rudeen

from Journeys Through Bookland.

BIBLIOGRAPHY

FACING PAGE: *Rat skins. Photograph by Rosamond Wolff Purcell.*

BOOKS

Alcott, Louisa May. *Little Women*. Pennsylvania: The Franklin Library, 1982.

Ali, Ahmed. *Of Rats and Diplomats*. Hyderabad: Sangam Books, 1985.

Balzac, Honoré de. *A Harlot High and Low*. Translated by Rayner Heppenstall. First published 1839–47 as *Splendeurs et misères des courtisanes*. Harmondsworth: Penguin, 1970.

Baring-Gould, Sabine. "Bishop Hatto" in *Curious Myths of the Middle Ages*. Edited by Edward Hardy. London: Jupiter Books, 1977 (first published 1896).

Baring-Gould, Sabine. "The Piper of Hameln" in *Curious Myths of the Middle Ages*. Edited by Edward Hardy. London: Jupiter Books, 1977 (first published 1896).

Barnes, Julian. *Flaubert's Parrot*. London: Jonathan Cape, 1984.

Barnhart, Robert K., ed. *The Barnhart Dictionary of Etymology*. New York: The H.W. Wilson Co., 1988.

Bataille, Georges. *The Impossible: A Story of Rats*. Translated by Robert Hurley. San Francisco: City Lights Books, 1991.

Baudelaire, Charles. "The Pauper's Toy" in *Parisian Prowler: Le Spleen de Paris, petits poèmes en prose*. Translated by Edward K. Kaplan. Atlanta: The University of Georgia Press, 1989.

Beckwith, Martha Warren. *Jamaica Folk-lore*. New York: The American Folk-Lore Society, 1928.

Bergen, Fanny D., ed. "Dreams: Animals" in *Current Superstitions: Collected from the Oral Tradition of English Speaking Folk*. The American Folk-Lore Society. Boston: Houghton, Mifflin & Co. 1896.

Bianco, José. *The Rats*. Translated by Daniel Balderston. Pittsburgh: Latin American Literary Review Press, 1983.

Boswell, James. *The Life of Samuel Johnson*. London: Everyman's Library (J.M. Dent & Sons Ltd.), 1976.

Brandon, Elizabeth. "Folk Medicine in French Louisiana" in *American Folk Medicine: A Symposium*. Edited by Wayland D. Hand. Berkeley: University of California Press, 1973.

Brewer's Dictionary of Phrase & Fable, Vol. 2. London: Cassell and Co., Ltd., 1903.

Browning, Robert. "The Pied Piper of Hamelin" in *The Poetical Works of Robert Browning*. London: Oxford University Press, 1940.

Brunvand, Jan Harold. *The Mexican Pet*. New York: W.W. Norton & Co., 1988.

Cagney, James. *Cagney by Cagney*. Garden City: Doubleday, 1976.

Cameron, Anne. *Wedding Cakes, Rats and Rodeo Queens*. Toronto: Harper Collins, 1994.

Camus, Albert. *The Plague*. Translated by Stuart Gilbert. Harmondsworth: Penguin, 1948.

Chambers Book of Days: A Miscellany of Popular Antiquities. 2 vols., edited by R. Chambers. London: W& R Chambers Ltd., 1862–64.

Chase, A.W. *Dr Chase's Third, Last and Complete Receipt Book*. Detroit: F.B. Dickerson & Co., 1890.

Chetwynd, Tom. *Dictionary of Symbols*. London: Aquarium, 1993.

Chiniquy, Charles. *Le Bon Dieu de Rome mangé par les rats*. Microfiche of a copy of the original edition found at the Bibliothèque de la Ville de Montréal, c. 1876.

Clavell, James. *King Rat*. © 1962 by James Clavell. New York: Fawcett World Library, 1962.

Combe, Jacques. *Jerome Bosch*. Paris: Editions Pierre Tisné, 1957.

Conly, Jane Leslie. *Racso and the Rats of NIMH*. New York: Harper & Row, 1986.

Conly, Jane Leslie. *R-T, Margaret, and the Rats of NIMH*. New York: Harper & Row, 1990.

Cortázar, Julio. *Hopscotch*. Translated by Gregory Rabassa. First published as "Rayuela." Toronto: Signet Books, 1967.

Cortázar, Julio. "Tara" in *Unreasonable Hours*. Translated by Alberto Manguel. © 1983 by Julio Cortázar and the heirs of Julio Cortázar. Translation © 1995 by Alberto Manguel. Toronto: Coach House Press, 1995. Reprinted by permission of Alberto Manguel and the Agencia Literaria Carmen Balcells.

Cowan, Jill Sanchia. *Kalila Wa Dimna: An Animal Allegory of the Mongol Court*. New York: Oxford University Press, 1989.

Coward, Noël. *The Rat Trap: A Play in Four Acts*. London: Ernest Benn Ltd., 1924.

Dansel, Michel. *Nos frères les rats*. Paris: Fayard, 1977.

Defoe, Daniel. *Journal of the Plague Year*. New York: Everyman's Library, 1966.

Delillo, Don. *White Noise*. New York: Viking, 1985.

Dibdin, Michael. *Ratking*. © 1988 by Michael Dibdin. London: Faber and Faber, 1988.

Dickinson, Emily. *Selected Poems and Letters of Emily Dickinson*. Edited by Robert N. Linscott. © 1959 by Robert N. Linscott. New York: Doubleday, 1959. Reprinted by permission of the estate of Robert N. Linscott.

Dickinson, Peter. *A Box of Nothing*. New York: Delacorte Press, 1988.

Dols, Michael W. *The Black Death in the Middle East*. Princeton: Princeton University Press, 1977.

Don Marquis. "freddy the rat perishes," from *archy and mehitabel* by Don Marquis. Copyright © 1927 by Doubleday, a division of Bantam, Doubleday, Dell Publishing Group, Inc. Reprinted by permission of Doubleday, a division of Bantam Doubleday Dell Publishing Group, Inc.

Doughty, C.M. *Passages from Arabia Deserta*. Harmondsworth: Penguin, 1956.

Durrell, Lawrence. *Balthazar*. London: Faber and Faber, 1962.

Durrell, Lawrence. *Justine*. London: Faber and Faber, 1962.

111

Durrell, Lawrence. *Pope Joan: translated and adapted from the Greek of Emmanuel Royidis*. Rev. ed. Woodstock, New York: The Overlook Press, 1960.

Eberhard, Wolfram. *A Dictionary of Chinese Symbols: Hidden Symbols in Chinese Life and Thought*. Translated by G. L. Campbell. London: Routledge, 1986.

Eberhard, Wolfram. *Folktales of China*. Chicago: University of Chicago Press, 1965.

Eliot, T.S. "The Waste Land" in *Collected Poems: 1909-1935*. London: Faber & Faber, 1936.

Farrell, Henry. *Whatever Happened to Baby Jane?* New York: Rinehart and Co., 1960.

Faulkner, William. *The Reivers*. New York: Random House, 1962.

Faulkner, William. *Sanctuary*. New York: The Modern Library, 1958.

Fitzgibbon, Constantine. *The Rat Report*. London: Constable, 1980.

Flaubert, Gustave. *Flaubert in Egypt: A Sensibility on Tour*. Translated and edited by Francis Steegmuller. Chicago: Academy Chicago Ltd., 1979.

Fleming, Ian. *From Russia with Love*. London: Pan Books, 1959.

Frazer, James George. *The Golden Bough: A Study in Magic and Religion*. Abridged ed. London: Macmillan and Co., 1959.

Garratt, John G. *Model Soldiers: A Collector's Guide*. 2nd ed. London: Seeley, 1971.

Gay, Peter, ed. "Notes Upon a Case of Obsessional Neurosis ("Rat Man") and Process Notes for the Case History" in *The Freud Reader*. New York: W. W. Norton & Co., 1989.

Gentle, Mary. *Rats and Gargoyles*. New York: Viking, 1991.

Ghosh, Amitav. "The Imam and the Indian" in *Granta Travel*. London: Granta, 1991.

Goethe, Johann Wolfgang von. *Faust*, Part 1. Translated by Thomas E. Webb. Dublin: Hodges, Figgis & Co., 1880.

Gordon, Karen Elizabeth, Barbara Hodgson and Nick Bantock. *Paris Out of Hand*. San Francisco: Chronicle Books, 1996.

Goyen, William. *The House of Breath*. New York: Random House, 1950.

Grahame, Kenneth. *The Wind in the Willows*. Illustrated by Ernest H. Shepard. 51st ed. London: Methuen & Co. Ltd., 1936 (first published 1908).

Grass, Günter. *The Rat*. Excerpts from *The Rat* by Günter Grass, English translation by Ralph Manheim. Copyright © 1987 by Harcourt Brace and Company. Reprinted by permission of Harcourt Brace and Company.

Graves, Robert. *The Greek Myths*, Vol. 1. Rev. ed. Harmondsworth: Penguin, 1960.

Greene, Barbara. *Too Late to Turn Back: Barbara and Graham Greene in Liberia*. London: Settle Bendall, 1981 (first published as *Land Benighted*, 1938).

Greene, Graham. *Journey without Maps*. London: Heinemann and Bodley Head, 1978 (first published 1936).

Grube, Ernst J., ed. *A Mirror for Princes from India*. Bombay: Marg Publications, 1991.

Guthrie, Woody. *Bound for Glory*. New York: Plume, 1983 (first published 1943).

Halliwell, Leslie, and John Walker. *Halliwell's Film Guide*. Revised and updated. New York: HarperCollins, 1995.

Hart, Martin. *Rats*. Translated by Arnold J. Pomerans. London: Allison & Busby, 1973. Reprinted by permission of Maartin 't Hart and Arnold J. Pomerans.

Hayden, Julie. "Day-Old Baby Rats" in *The Lists of the Past*. Viking: New York, 1976.

Hébert, François. "Le rat dans la bibliothèque" in *Le dernier chant de l'avant-dernier dodo*. Translated by Karen Elizabeth Gordon. © Les Editions du Roseau. Montreal: Collection Garamond, 1986. Reprinted by permission of François Hébert and Karen Elizabeth Gordon.

Herlihy, James Leo. *Midnight Cowboy*. St. Albans: Triad/Panther Books, 1977.

Herodotus. *The Histories*. Translated by Aubrey de Sélincourt. Harmondsworth: Penguin, 1965.

Higgins, George V. *The Rat on Fire*. New York: Alfred A. Knopf, 1981.

Homel, David. *Rat Palms*. Toronto: HarperCollins Publishers Ltd., 1992.

Hood, Thomas. *Tom Tucker and Little Bo-Peep*. New York: Cassell Pub. Co., 1891.

Hudson, Lionel. *The Rats of Rangoon: The Inside Story of the 'Fiasco' That Took Place at the End of the War in Burma*. London: Arrow Books, 1989.

Hugo, Victor. *The Hunchback of Notre Dame*. Translated by Walter J. Cobb. New York: Signet Classics, 1965.

Hugo, Victor. *Les Misérables*. Translated by Isabel F. Hapgood. London: The Walter Scott Publishing Co. Ltd., 1908.

Joyce, James. *Ulysses*. Harmondsworth: Penguin Books, 1972.

Jullian, Philippe. *Montmartre*. Translated by Anne Carter. Oxford: Phaidon, 1977.

King, Stephen. "Graveyard Shift" in *Night Shift*. New York: Doubleday, 1978.

Kinglake, A.W. *Eothen*. London: Century Publishing Co., Ltd., 1982.

Kosinski, Jerzy. *The Painted Bird*. New York: Bantam Books, 1978.

Kotzwinkle, William. *Doctor Rat*. New York: Knopf, 1976.

Langland, William. *Piers the Plowman*. Translated by Margaret Williams. New York: Random House, 1971.

Lau, Theodora. *The Handbook of Chinese Horoscopes*. New York: Harper & Row, 1993.

Lenaghan, R.T., ed. *Caxton's Aesop*. Cambridge: Harvard University Press, 1967.

Latham, Robert Gordon, *A Dictionary of the English Language*. London: Longmans, Green & Co., 1882.

Lautréamont, Comte de. *Maldoror*. Translated by Paul Knight. Harmondsworth: Penguin, 1978.

Leroux, Gaston. *The Phantom of the Opera*. First published 1910 as *Le fantôme de l'opéra* by Lafitte, Paris. London: Michael O'Mara Books Ltd., 1987.

Lewis, Wyndham. *Malign Fiesta*. London: Jupiter Books/John Calder, 1966.

Lewis, Wyndham. *Monstre Gai*. Jupiter Books/John Calder, 1965.

Lorenz, Konrad. *On Aggression*. Translated by Marjorie Kerr Wilson. New York: Harcourt, Brace & World, Inc., 1966.

Lovecraft, H.P. "Rats in the Wall" in *The Dunwich Horror and Others*. Selected by August Derleth. Sauk City, Wisc.: Arkham House, n.d. (first published 1924 by Rural Publishing Corp. for *Weird Tales*).

Lovecraft, H.P. "Under the Pyramid" in *Dagon and Other Macabre Tales*. Sauk City, Wisc: Arkham House Publishers, Inc., n.d.

McCullers, Carson. *The Heart Is a Lonely Hunter*. Boston: Houghton Mifflin Co., 1967.

McKendry, John J. *Aesop: Five Centuries of Illustrated Fables*. New York: The Metropolitan Museum of Art, 1964.

Malet, Léo. *The Rats of Montsouris*. Translated by Peter Hudson. Pan Books. London: 1991.

Mallis, Arnold. *Handbook of Pest Control*, 6th ed. Cleveland: Franzak & Foster Co., 1982.

Mansfield, M.T. "Chinese Superstition" in *The Folk-lore Journal*, Vol. V (January-December 1887). London: Elliot Stock, 1887.

Marsh, Ngaio. *Death at the Bar*. London: William Collins & Sons, 1986.

Matthiessen, F.O., and Russell Cheney. *Rat & The Devil: Journal Letters of F.O. Matthiessen and Russell Cheney*. Edited by Louis Hyde. © 1978 by Louis Hyde.

Hamden, Conn.: Archon Books, 1978. Reprinted by permission of the Shoe String Press, Inc.

Matthiessen, Peter. *Under the Mountain Wall: A Chronicle of Two Seasons in Stone Age New Guinea*. London: Penguin, 1987.

Meehan, Bernard. *The Book of Kells*. London: Thames & Hudson, 1994.

Mitchell, Joseph. "The Rats on the Waterfront" in *The Bottom of the Harbor*. First published as "Thirty-two Rats from Casablanca" in *The New Yorker*, April 29, 1944. © 1987 by Joseph Mitchell. New York: The Modern Library, 1987. Reprinted by permission of Random House, Inc.

Moseley, H.N. *Notes by a Naturalist on the Challenger*. London: Macmillan, 1879.

Murphy, Dervla. *Muddling Through in Madagascar*. London: Century Publishing Co. Ltd., 1986.

Nabokov, Vladimir. *Ada or Ardor: A Family Chronicle*. New York: McGraw-Hill Book Co., 1969.

Nikiforuk, Andrew. *The Fourth Horseman*. Toronto: Viking, 1991.

O'Brien, Robert C. *Mrs. Frisby and the Rats of NIMH*. New York: Atheneum, 1971.

Official Handbook of the Territory of New Guinea. Canberra: L.F. Johnston, Commonwealth Government Printer, 1943.

Okri, Ben. *The Famished Road*. London: Vintage, 1992.

Ondaatje, Michael. *Rat Jelly*. © 1973 by Michael Ondaatje. Toronto: Coach House Press, 1973. Reprinted by permission of Michael Ondaatje.

O'Neill, James. *Terror on Tape*. New York: Billboard Books, 1994.

Orwell, George. *Burmese Days*. New York: Harcourt Brace Jovanovich, 1962.

Orwell, George. *Down and Out in Paris and London*. Harmondsworth: Penguin, 1974.

Orwell, George. *Homage to Catalonia*. New York: Harcourt Brace Jovanovich, 1962.

Orwell, George. *Nineteen Eighty-four*. London: Secker & Warburg, 1949.

Osborne, Lawrence. *Paris Dreambook: An Unconventional Guide to the Splendor and Squalor of the City*. New York: Pantheon, 1991.

O'Sullivan, Sean, ed. and trans. *Folktales of Ireland*. Chicago: University of Chicago Press, 1966.

Painter, George D. *Proust: The Later Years*. Boston: Little, Brown and Co., 1965.

Peake, Mervyn. *Gormenghast*. Harmondsworth: Penguin Modern Classics, 1969 (first published 1950).

Pliny the Elder. *Pliny's Natural History: Selections from the History of the World*. Edited and selected by Paul Turner. London: Centaur Press Ltd., 1962.

Poe, Edgar Allan. "The Pit and the Pendulum" in *The Work of Edgar Allan Poe*. London: Oxford University Press, 1927 (first published 1843).

Porter, J.R., and W.M.S. Russell. *Animals in Folklore*. Cambridge: D.S. Brewer Ltd. and Rowman & Littlefield for The Folklore Society, 1978.

Puhvel, Jaan. "The Mole in Folk Medicine" in *American Folk Medicine: A Symposium*. Edited by Wayland D. Hand. Berkeley: University of California Press, 1973.

Rabelais, François. *Gargantua and Pantagruel*. Translated by Sir Thomas Urquhart and Peter Motteux. N.p.: Encyclopaedia Britannica, Inc., 1952.

Radford, E., and M. A. Radford. *Encyclopaedia of Superstitions*. Revised and edited by Christina Hold. London: Hutchinson, 1961.

Rambaud, Patrick. *Comme des rats*. Paris: Bernard Grasset, 1980.

Rawlinson, George. *History of Ancient Egypt*. London: Longmans, Green, and Co., 1881.

Reid, Donald. *Paris Sewers and Sewermen*. Cambridge: Harvard University Press, 1991.

Remarque, Erich Maria. *All Quiet on the Western Front*. Cutchogue, New York: Buccaneer Books, 1983.

Ridley, Philip. *In the Eyes of Mister Fury*. London: Penguin, 1989.

Robinson, Edward Arlington. "The Rat," from *Selected Poems of Edward Arlington Robinson*. New York: The Macmillan Co., 1937. Reprinted by permission of Simon & Schuster.

Romanes, George J. *Animal Intelligence*. London: Kegan Paul, Trench, Trübner & Co., 1904.

Romanowski, Patricia, and Holly George-Warren, eds. *The New Rolling Stone Encyclopedia of Rock & Roll*. New York: Fireside, 1995.

Shadbolt, Doris. *Travel Diary of India*. Unpublished, unpaginated, 1974–75.

Shakespeare, William. *As You Like It*.

Shakespeare, William. *Hamlet*.

Shakespeare, William. *King Lear*.

Shakespeare, William. *Macbeth*.

Shakespeare, William. *The Merchant of Venice*.

Shakespeare, William. *The Merry Wives of Windsor*.

Shakespeare, William. *Romeo and Juliet*.

Shakespeare, William. *The Tempest*.

Shrewsbury, J.F.D. *A History of Bubonic Plague*. Cambridge: Cambridge University Press, 1970.

Sillitoe, Alan. *The Rats and Other Poems*. © 1960 by Alan Sillitoe. London: W.J. Allen, 1960. Reprinted by permission of Alan Sillitoe.

Simenon, Georges. *Maigret à l'école*. Paris: Presses de la Cité, 1968.

Smith, Geddes. *Plague on Us*. New York: The Commonwealth Fund, 1941.

Sorrentino, Gilbert. *Splendide-Hôtel*. © 1984 by Gilbert Sorrentino. Normal, Illinois: The Dalkey Archive Press, 1984. Reprinted by permission of the Dalkey Archive Press.

Spiller, Sam. "The Great Plague of Bronston," in *Stories of Men and Rats*. Smithtown, New York: Exposition Press, 1982.

Stoker, Bram. "The Burial of the Rats" in *Dracula's Guest and Other Weird Stories*. Mattituck, New York: Amereon House, 1990 (first published 1914).

Stoker, Bram. *Dracula*. Harmondsworth: Penguin, 1993 (first published 1897).

Stoker, Bram. "The Judge's House" in *Dracula's Guest and Other Weird Stories*. Mattituck, New York: Amereon House, 1990 (first published 1914).

Stout, Earl J. *Folklore from Iowa*. New York: The American Folk-lore Society, 1936.

Swift, Jonathan. *Gulliver's Travels*. London: Pitman, 1871 (first published 1726).

Terry, Philip, T. *Terry's Guide to the Japanese Empire: Including Korea and Formosa, A Handbook for Travelers*. New York: Houghton Mifflin Co., 1920.

Thérien, Giles. *Ratopolis*. Montreal: Les presses de l'université du Québec, 1977.

Theroux, Alexander. "Mister Snickup's Cloak" in *Darconville's Cat*. Garden City: Doubleday & Co., 1981.

Tournier, Michel. *Gemini*. First published in 1975 as *Les météores* by Editions Gallimard. Translated by Anne Carter. London: Methuen, 1985.

Twain, Mark. *The Adventures of Tom Sawyer*. Garden City: International Collectors Library, n.d. (first published 1876).

Twigg, Graham. *The Brown Rat*. London: David & Charles, 1975.

Van de Wetering, Janwillem. *The Rattle-Rat*. New York: Pantheon, 1985.

Wells, H.G. *The Food of the Gods*. London: Collins, 1955 (first published 1904).

West, Paul. *Rat Man of Paris*. Garden City, New York: Doubleday, 1986.

Westermarck, Edward. *Ritual and Belief in Morocco*. London: Macmillan and Co., 1926.

Wilson, F.P. *The Plague in Shakespeare's London*. London: Oxford University Press, 1963 (first published 1927).

Wood, Rev J.G. *The Boy's Own Book of Natural History*. London: George Routledge & Sons, n.d. (late 1800s).

Woolrich, Cornell (writing as William Irish). *I Married a Dead Man*. Harmondsworth: Penguin Books, 1982.

Wright, Elizur, trans. *Jean de la Fontaine: The Fables*. London: Jupiter Books, 1975.

Zaniewski, Andrzej. *Rat*. Translated by Ewa Hryniewicz-Yarbrough. New York: Arcade Publishing, 1994.

Ziegler, Philip. *The Black Death*. Dover, New Hampshire: Alan Sutton, 1991.

Zinsser, Hans. *Rats, Lice and History*. © 1934, 1935 by Hans Zinsser, © renewed 1963 by Dr. Hans Zinsser. Boston: Little, Brown and Co., 1963. Reprinted by permission of Little, Brown and Company.

PERIODICALS

Allis, Sam. "The Rats Are Coming," *Time*, February 17, 1989.

Barber, John. "Budget cutting lets rats run free," *Globe and Mail*, March 16, 1995.

"Better Than Spinach," *Discover*, April 1995.

"The Big Boys," *The New Yorker*, September 28, 1992.

Callo, Kathleen. "Hanoi's Metropole hotel kicks out the rats," *Globe and Mail*, November 28, 1992.

Canby, Thomas Y. "The Rat: Lapdog of the Devil," *National Geographic*, July 1977.

Clark, Victoria. "Rats thrive in Bucharest's market economy," *Montreal Gazette* (reprinted from the London *Observer*), November 16, 1992.

Colors Magazine, no. 7, n.d., p. 125.

"Curiosity sucks life out of rats," *Globe and Mail* (reprinted from the *Economist*), January 7, 1995.

"Dead Rats Among Debris Plaguing Wind-Surfers," *Calgary Herald*, July 15, 1992.

Discover, untitled, April 1995.

Duplaix, Nicole. "Fleas: The Lethal Leapers," *National Geographic*, May 1988.

Goodspeed, Peter. "Range-fed rats top Guangzhou menu," *Toronto Star*, October 27, 1992.

Gutfeld, Rose. "Of All Those Rats in Washington, D.C., Most are Rodents," *Wall Street Journal*, November 24, 1992.

"High-flying rat traps," *Globe and Mail*, February 19, 1992.

Kesterton, Michael. "The patter of feet," *Globe and Mail*, July 17, 1995.

"Man Kept Pet Rats," Vancouver *Province*, June 30, 1995.

Mason, Robert Lee. "Wile E. Coyote moves to the big smoke," *Globe and Mail*, February 3, 1996.

"Millionaire loses rat-catching job," *Globe and Mail*, July 17, 1995.

Nemeth, Mary. "Rats on the run," *Maclean's*, August 8, 1994.

Newman, Steve. "Earthweek: A diary of the planet." *Vancouver Sun*, August 17, 1996.

Schactman, Ken, and Danny Savello. "Roger Redux," *Scarlet Street*, Fall 1995.

"Watching popular newsroom sitcom is like swallowing putrid rats—Chinese newspaper," *Montreal Gazette*, March 8, 1992.

Weiss, Rick. "Rats, Mice, Birds: They're not Animals?" *Washington Post*, July 5, 1994.

Witt, Howard. "Vladivostok a nightmare: City overrun by crooks, rats and corruption," *Winnipeg Free Press*, November 22, 1994.

Yoder, Stephen Kreider. "Rats' nests yield store of tiny domestic treasures," *Globe and Mail* (reprinted from the *Wall Street Journal*), March 25, 1995.

Yoshikawa, Miho. "Tokyo's main streets hide gnawing problem," *Globe and Mail*, November 28, 1994.

INTERVIEWS

Lemercier, Jean-Paul. Service de lutte contre les rongeurs, Paris, February, 1996. Interview by Françoise Giovannangeli.

Vétil, Roland. Section de lutte contre les rongeurs, Paris, February, 1996. Interview by Françoise Giovannangeli.

Winn, Mr. Public Health Department, Washington, D.C., February, 1996. Interview by Barbara Smith.

IMAGE SOURCES *See also specific captions*

Pp. 51, 79, 89, 108, 160: Applebaum, Stanley. *Fantastic Illustrations of Grandville*, New York: Dover Publications Ltd., 1974.

P. 95: Borthwich, Rev J. Douglas. *History of Montreal and Commercial Register*. Montreal: Gebhardt-Berthiaume Lithographic and Printing Co., 1885.

Pp. 42, 46, 79, 106: *Catchpenny Prints: 163 Popular Engravings from the Eighteenth Century*. New York: Dover Publications Ltd., 1970.

Pp. 24, 38: *Encyclopædia Britannica*, ninth edition. Edinburgh: Adams and Charles Black, 1878.

Pp. 30, 31: *Fabulos de Esopo*. Facsimile ed. of 1489 edition. Madrid: Topgrafia de Archivos, 1929.

Pp. 6, 49, 60, 104: Grafton, Carol Belanger, ed. *Doré Spot Illustrations: A Treasury from his Masterworks*. New York: Dover Publications Ltd., 1987.

P. 9: Grahame, Kenneth. *The Wind in the Willows*. Illustrated by Ernest H. Shepard. 51st ed. London: Methuen & Co. Ltd., 1936.

Pp. 36–37: *Guerre des rats et des grenouilles*. Paris: Guérin-Müller et Cie, c. 1890.

P. 81: Harter, Jim. *Animals*. New York: Dover Publications Ltd., 1979.

P. 109: Hood, Thomas. *Tom Tucker and Little Bo-Peep*. Illustrated by Alice Wheaton Adams. New York: Cassell Publishing Co., 1891.

P. 43: Hutchinson, Robert, ed. *1800 Woodcuts by Thomas Bewick and His School*. New York: Dover Publications Ltd., 1962.

Pp. ix, 33, 38, 77: La Fontaine, J. de. *Fables de J. de la Fontaine. Illustrées de 120 Gravures par J. Desandré et W.H. Freeman*. Paris: Bernardin-Béchet, 1882.

Pp. 1, 9, 33, 34, 76: La Fontaine, J. de. *Fables de la Fontaine. Illustrations par J.J. Grandville*. Paris: Garnier Frères, 1859.

P. 93: Mendenhall, John. *French Trademarks*. San Francisco: Chronicle Books, © 1991. Reprinted by permission of Chronicle Books.

P. 40: *1,000 Quaint Cuts*. New York: The Art Direction Book Co., 1973.

Pp. 2, 86, 87, 88, 89, 94, 95: *Official Gazetteer of the U.S. Patent Office*, 1850–1920.

P. 41: Perrault, Charles. "The Master Cat, or Puss in Boots" in *Perrault's Fairy Tales*. New York: Dover Publications Ltd., 1989.

P. 70: Skal, David J. *Hollywood Gothic: The Tangled Web of Dracula from Novel to Stage to Screen*. © 1990 by Visual Cortex Ltd. New York: W.W. Norton & Co., 1990. Reprinted by permission of David J. Skal.

INDEX

116